Still BEAUTIFUL

FLAWS AND ALL

A STORY OF BROKENNESS.

A STORY OF RESILIENCE, SELF-LOVE, AND
BECOMING UNAPOLOGETICALLY YOU

CHARMAYNE HARRELL

ISBN # 979-8-9998448-3-5

# Dedication

To every soul quietly fighting battles no one sees— those wrestling with addiction, trauma, abuse, shame, or the cycles you never chose to endure, but life threw at you.

This book is for you. You are not alone, and your story is still unfolding.

To the loved ones who stand quietly in the background, watching their loved ones slowly fade away, praying, hoping, and believing, even when it feels like nothing will change—this is for you too. This is also for those who rose above the circumstance and beat addiction, and for the family members who watched their loved ones fight and overcome—this is for you too.

To those whose lives were taken too soon by addiction, trauma, abuse, or suicide — may your souls rest in peace. You are remembered, and you are not forgotten.

May these pages remind us all that even in brokenness, there is beauty, even in darkness, there is light, and even in struggle, there is hope.

With love,
Charmayne

 **Contents**

Introduction - **1**

Chapter 1 : Born into Brokenness - **12**

Chapter 2: Chasing Love in All the Wrong Places - **21**

Chapter 3 : The Essence of Grace - **26**

Chapter 4 : The Mirror of My Pain - **30**

Chapter 5 : East Side Chronicles - **34**

Chapter 6 : The Price of Loyalty - **40**

Chapter 7 : All While Chasing Shadows - **45**

Chapter 8 : Love in Its Purest Form - **50**

Chapter 9 : Deliverance in the Midst of Chaos - **53**

Chapter 10 : High Stakes, Empty Tanks - **59**

Chapter 11 : Addicted to Chaos - **64**

Chapter 12 : The Price of Comfort - **68**

Chapter 13 : The Moment My Soul Cried Out - **72**

Chapter 14 : December 4, 2020—The Day of Redemption - **77**

Chapter 15 : I'm No Longer Your Favorite Version - **82**

Chapter 16 : The Battles in My Mind - **88**

Chapter 17 : When Freedom Isn't Enough - **91**

Chapter 18 : Redirection, Not Rejection - **95**

Chapter 19 : Lessons in Detours - **99**

Chapter 20 : Shadows of Wanting - **103**

Chapter 21 : Surrender - **107**

Chapter 22 : Maintaining Recovery - **113**

Special Shout-Out - **119**

# Introduction

I never thought my story mattered. For years, I carried shame that nobody could see—heavy, quiet, buried deep. Every mistake, every heartbreak, every scar felt like proof that I wasn't enough.

But here's the truth: Every fall, every wrong turn, every time I thought I couldn't rise—I did. I survived. I fought. I kept going.

And in the middle of all the chaos, all the pain, all the nights I wanted to give up—I found beauty. Not because I was flawless, but because I was real. Because each scar tells a story, each mistake carved a lesson, each struggle made me stronger.

This is my story—raw, unfiltered, and real.
Still beautiful. Flaws and all.

# A Message of Hope

To all the beautiful souls reading this, whether you feel broken, whether you're still struggling with acceptance, abuse, addiction, or any kind of pain:

I want you to know that your story matters. YOU matter.

Even in your darkest moments, there is hope. Healing is possible, even when it feels impossible. Writing my story has shown me that every tear, every mistake, every triumph—they all become steps toward freedom.

As I put my truth on paper, I feel healing happening one word at a time. Every sentence is a chance to understand myself. Every chapter serves as a reminder of the lessons, the struggles, and the triumphs that shape who I am.

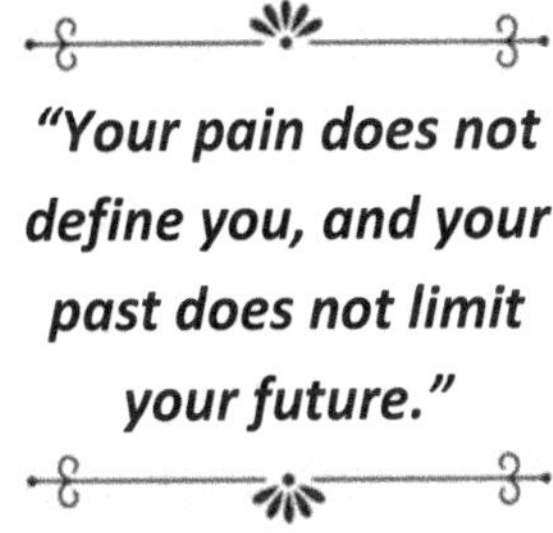

If my journey can remind you that broken pieces can be made whole, then know this: You, too, can be made whole. Your pain does not define you, and your past does not limit your future.

And, my loves . . . forgive yourself. Forgive yourself for not knowing. Forgive yourself for the lies you believed. Forgive yourself for the times you hurt others and for the times you hurt yourself. Forgive yourself for being human, for making mistakes, for learning the hard way. Forgiveness is not about letting anyone else off the hook—it's about freeing your own heart.

Keep going. Keep believing. Keep choosing yourself.

A Word of Encouragement

Sometimes we get frustrated with God for how our lives have turned out, or even for the pain and hardships we've endured. It's easy to question why certain things happened, why people hurt us, or why we hurt ourselves, or why our lives didn't go the way we planned. But the truth is, everything God allows has a purpose. Nothing in our journey is wasted—even the struggles that seem unbearable in the moment.

It's in the struggles, the heartbreak, the mistakes, and the healing that we learn who we really are and what we are capable of.

If you're reading this and feeling broken, lost, or like it's too late, know this: *It's not too late*. It's never too late for your family, your loved ones, or yourself. You can still reclaim your life, forgive yourself, and walk into a future filled with hope—but you have to want it. You can still choose love over fear, healing over hurt, and faith over doubt.

Your past doesn't define you. Your mistakes don't disqualify you. God's grace is bigger than your pain, stronger than your fears, and deeper than your regrets. There is freedom waiting for you, and it begins the moment you open your heart to it, just like I did.

So breathe. Trust the process. Keep moving forward. Your redemption, your healing, your second chance—it's already on the way.

Bondage

Bondage is more than chains you can see. It's being trapped by fear, addiction, pain, trauma, abuse, or a toxic relationship. It's the invisible force that keeps your mind, heart, and spirit from feeling free. Bondage holds you in patterns of hurt and prevents you from stepping fully into who you were created to be.

But bondage is not permanent. Recognizing it is the first step toward breaking free. True freedom begins when you face the truth, reach for help, and allow healing to take root—even in the places you thought were lost. It's also acknowledging that something is wrong and refusing to ignore it.

> *"You can be free from bondage—but you have to choose yourself, set boundaries, and reclaim your life."*

You can be free from bondage—but you have to choose yourself, set boundaries, and reclaim your life. The chains may feel heavy, but the first step toward your liberation is realizing that your story does not end in captivity—it ends in freedom.

Message: Do Not Judge

"Do not judge, or you too will be judged. For in the same way you judge others, you will be judged, and with the measure you use, it will be measured to you" (Matthew 7:1–2 NIV).

As I share my story, I want to remind all who are reading: Judgment can be a dangerous trap. It's easy to look at someone else's life and criticize, to shake your head at their choices, their mistakes, their addictions, their pain. I was that little girl—judging my family, my parents, even those who sold drugs to the people I loved. I thought I

knew better, that I was immune to the patterns I
condemned.

But God showed me in the hardest way that when we
judge, we set ourselves up to experience the very same
lessons, often in a deeper and more painful way.
Addiction, betrayal, heartbreak—these are not
punishments but mirrors. They reflect the hearts of those
we judged and force us to confront our own brokenness.

This is not to excuse mistakes but to understand them.
God allows us to walk in experiences we once condemned
so we can learn, grow, and develop compassion. It's a
reminder that nobody is beyond grace, and that life is a
journey to understanding, not to condemning.

So before you judge, remember: The measure you use will
come back to you. Extend mercy. Extend patience. Extend
understanding. And know that God can use even the most
painful lessons to shape you into someone stronger, wiser,
and more compassionate than you ever imagined.

The question to ask ourselves daily is: *Am I walking in love,
or am I judging the shadows I don't fully understand?*

The Truth About Sexual Sin

Let's be honest—sexual sin is one of those things people
don't like to talk about anymore. But the truth is, it's

destroying more souls, more families, and more destinies than we're willing to admit. And this isn't about shame; it's about awareness.

We live in a world that makes it easy to give our bodies away and call it freedom, when in reality, it's bondage. Every time we connect ourselves with someone, we're not just sharing a physical moment—we're exchanging energy, emotions, and even spirits. Some of us are walking around carrying things that were never ours to carry, all because we laid down with someone who was never meant to touch us.

To my brothers and my sisters—whether you've lived wild, whether you've made mistakes, whether you've contracted something or walked away untouched—this message is for all of us. None of us are better than the other. Some got mercy in the form of a warning, and some got mercy in the form of survival. Either way, it was still mercy.

This is not about perfection; it's about protection. God gave us boundaries not to restrict us, but to save us—to keep our hearts, minds, and bodies safe from what was designed to destroy us.

So love yourself enough to pause before you give yourself away. Love yourself enough to ask, "What will this cost me?" Because your body is not just skin and bone—it's a temple, a vessel, a home for God's Spirit. And if you've already crossed that line, don't drown in guilt. Repentance is not about reliving the shame; it's about receiving forgiveness and walking in wisdom.

Sexual sin doesn't define you—but it can destroy you if you keep ignoring the warning signs. So choose better. Choose you. Choose life. And thank God for the grace that gives us another chance to start over—covered, forgiven, and free.

Understanding an Addict Mentality

An addict mentality isn't just about substance abuse—it's a mindset, a way of thinking and reacting to life that keeps you trapped in cycles of dependency. It doesn't always have to be drugs. It can be people, validation, or unhealthy patterns. It's the part of you that constantly seeks something outside of yourself to feel whole, to numb the pain, or to experience joy, even when the substance or behavior is gone.

This mindset can linger if it hasn't been addressed and healed. Often, it's tied to not knowing your worth. When you spend years giving yourself away—emotionally, mentally, or physically—you can lose sight of your own value. Not knowing your worth, combined with never having someone show you what true love is while growing up, can make this even more complicated. Trauma from your past also plays a role, shaping how you feel, think, and respond to love, boundaries, and trust.

An addict mentality convinces you that you need someone or something else to feel complete, leaving the real work of self-love and healing untouched. Breaking free isn't just about walking away from harmful behaviors or substances; it's about learning to see your own value, respecting yourself, and practicing forgiveness toward yourself. Until you do that, the cycle can continue—often in new forms.

"True freedom comes when you replace the craving for external validation with the knowledge of your own worth."

True freedom comes when you replace the craving for external validation with the knowledge of your own worth.

Sneak Peek: Dear Me

Why must we hurt ourselves—
sometimes with words, sometimes with choices,
sometimes by loving too little,
sometimes by loving too much?

Why must we learn the hard way
that the heart can be both fragile and fierce,
that mistakes are not the end,
but maps pointing to the lessons we refuse to see?

Why must we love, and lose,
and in the spaces in between,
find ourselves again?

Why must we look in the mirror
and face the parts we wanted to hide—
the behaviors that scared us,
the doubts that held us hostage?

And slowly,
we are learning to love the us
who fell,
who screamed,
who cried,
who survived.

Dear Me is having conversations with the soul we once ignored.

Inside, there are affirmations to ourselves,
along with poems and letters to the parts of us we neglected.

It is a reminder that even in our brokenness,
we are worthy of love, forgiveness, and understanding.

This book is for anyone who has loved too much,
hated too harshly,
and still keeps trying.

It is for all of us who want to stop hurting ourselves,
and start learning to hold our hearts gently.

Chapter 1

Born into Brokenness

I really don't know too much about my childhood, or the exact ages of everything that happened, but I'll give it to you the way I remember it.

From what I can recall, the chaos began around the time I was seven or eight and continued through my early teens, shaping the way I saw the world, the way I loved, and the way I survived.

I didn't ask to be born into brokenness—but I felt like I was.

I barely saw my father. He was rarely home, always working, chasing women, or lost in his addictions. When he would finally return after being gone for days, he brought gifts—brand-new washing machines, floor-model color TVs, cable—as if those things could replace the time he had missed. As if those things could fill the emptiness he left behind.

My mother was quiet. She loved to sit and rock us. She tried her best to comfort and nurture me and my siblings, but she was slowly fading away. She loved my father deeply, yet she grew tired of watching him run from woman to woman. In her desperation to keep him home, she tried the same monster that kept him away. And because he loved her in his own broken way, he gave it to her. She thought it would make him stay—but it didn't.

Now both of my parents were tangled in the grip of addiction, and their love was buried under the weight of their own pain.

I was about eight years old when I started realizing what body parts meant. I was never taught about good touch or bad touch, and somehow, bad touches became the norm from a close family member. I never told anyone, because that's how my parents were somehow able to afford their addictions.

As a kid, I went outside to play like any other child, but I noticed something about myself—I always played rough. I would ride my brother on the handlebars of my bike and slam on the brakes hard so he could fly off. I asked him if he wanted to fly, and when he said yes, I let him go. I tossed my baby sibling up in the air and let him fall to the floor. I would always fight with my other siblings— brothers and sisters—until they jumped me and slammed the table into my head.

When we played with shopping carts, we'd bend down the seat part and pretend they were limousines, crashing them into each other. One time, I pushed a friend in the cart really fast and just let her go—she ended up breaking her arm. Somehow, my anger, curiosity, and energy found their way out through rough play.

And eventually, that rough play caught up with me. One day, I slammed my hand into broken glass lying on the ground. The cut split my hand wide open.

I don't remember my mother being there, so my father rushed me to the hospital. I thought I was just going to get stitches.

Instead, the moment we arrived, everything changed. The nurses moved quickly, their voices loud, hands grabbing me. Before I could understand what was happening, they strapped me into a straitjacket like I was some kind of out-of-control child.

I wasn't afraid of the pain in my hand. I was afraid of being held down. Being restrained triggered something deep inside me, a fear I didn't yet have the words for. It was the same fear that came from other moments when people had pinned me down and taken my power away.

Suddenly I wasn't just a little girl with a cut hand. I was a child fighting to breathe. Somehow, I broke free. I remember running down the hospital hallway, blood dripping from my hand, nurses shouting behind me, my heart pounding in my chest. I wasn't running from the

injury. I was running from the feeling of being trapped
again.

Around the same time, maybe eight or nine, chaos broke
out at home. Several men came looking for my parents
because of money owed for drugs. Our back door window
was smashed out, fights broke out, and anger and fear
filled the air.

Instead of screaming and hiding, my siblings and I tried to
fight back. We thought we were protecting our parents—
or maybe just protecting ourselves.

The next day, I still had to go to school.

No one at school saw a little girl
trying to survive. They only saw
someone they could pick apart.
Some of the children even knew
what I was going through
because they lived in the same
apartment complex. Still, they
laughed and teased me anyway.
My clothes were sometimes dirty, even though we had a
washer. I didn't know how to use it. My hair was barely
done.

Sometimes I just wanted to disappear—or fight everyone.
Some days, I had to fight over sneakers that were mine,

and it ended with my face scratched up really, really bad. My favorite auntie, who has since passed away, brought me to her house. Her daughters, whom I consider my sisters more than cousins, did my hair. They gave me clothes and put makeup on me because they knew the next day was picture day. My aunt always called me her Mini-Me, and she said I couldn't go out looking crazy. That day, I felt beautiful and untouchable.

Sometimes I hid in my imagination.

That place was Care Bear Land. I would go into the closet, close my eyes, and talk to my imaginary friends. My Care Bears were like the only real friends I had. I talked to them about my day, about the abuse, about everything that hurt. No one could see me there. No one could laugh at me. No one could even find me. I could hear my siblings and my mom yelling my name, but even then, I was still unseen. For the first time, I felt a little safe.

But as a kid, there weren't always bad days. There were a lot of good memories too. Our annual church trip to Clementon Park was one of the best times of my childhood. Those days were full of laughter, running around with my sister and our friends all dressed alike. There were also times when a lady in the neighborhood sold the best ice creams and baked cookies, and everyone would scrape together change just to get a treat. Of course, there were the "bad kids" in the neighborhood—

the ones we were all scared of, just being kids the way kids can be. Then there were the kids you had crushes on, the secret kisses and adventures—like going to the Elks' home or exploring the graveyard. We couldn't wait for our parents to have company so we could run outside to play and enjoy ourselves. In those moments, it didn't matter what chaos waited at home; the world felt bright, free, and ours. For a little while, it was just fun, laughter, and the world feeling normal.

Eventually, my parents' pain became too heavy to carry. Foster care stepped in.

Before that, God sent us angels: my paternal grandmother, my father's sisters, and my mother's childhood friend, Aunt Josephine.

> **"Eventually, my parents' pain became too heavy to carry."**

They gave us what our parents couldn't: joy in small doses. Christmases. Birthdays. Little moments that became lifelines. I still hold on to those memories. They proved that love could exist even in the middle of chaos.

When DYFS stepped in, we were placed with relatives on my father's side. My parents were barely around, and addiction had taken almost everything from them.

The other kids in the house—their children, including one

of my siblings—had new clothes, went on outings, and received attention that showed someone cared.
I didn't. I existed in the background, overlooked, like I was just taking up space.

They were seen. I was tolerated.

That kind of invisibility cuts deeper than any wound. It teaches you, early on, that love has limits . . . and sometimes, you are the one people choose not to see.

The tension in that house didn't make sense. It felt like she carried something against me—envy, resentment, or her own insecurities. Suddenly I was treated like a problem instead of a child.

One day she had me examined by a doctor, accusing me of things I hadn't even thought about, even assuming I was messing with her boyfriend. I was only ten or eleven.

Sitting in that office, confused, embarrassed, scared, I wondered what I could have possibly done to make someone see me that way. The doctor told her there was nothing to be done—I had never even been touched. Instead of giving me peace, it gave me a different kind of hurt.

I walked out wondering why I wasn't protected, why anyone would look at a child like that, why I had to prove I wasn't guilty of things I didn't do. That kind of shame follows a child, even when it never belonged to them.

I felt like I was only tolerated for the check—not loved for the child I was.

So I learned to survive.

And survival didn't always look pretty. Sometimes it meant hurting myself or others just to be noticed. Sometimes it meant acting out in anger, because anger always got a reaction, even when love didn't. Eventually, I became labeled the "problem child."

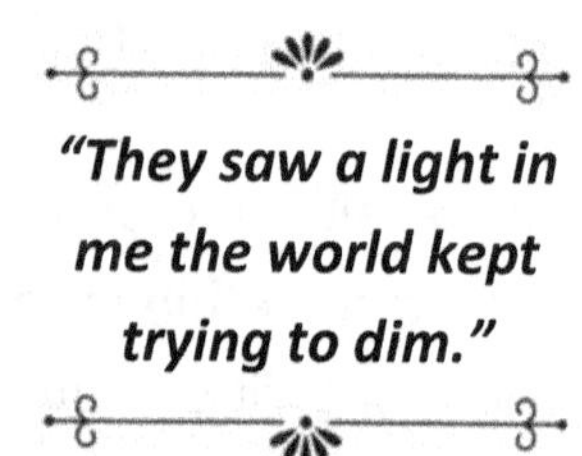

But there were two people who never treated me that way: my grandmother and my favorite aunt—my father's sister, the one everyone said I looked like.

They loved me without demanding silence or perfection. They saw a light in me the world kept trying to dim. They made me feel like I mattered.

Pain like that doesn't disappear just because a few people loved you right. It lingers. It whispers that maybe love isn't meant for you. And even when it shows up, it might not stay.

By eighth grade, that whisper had started to feel like truth.

When I graduated, none of the people I lived with showed up. Not even my sibling. Only my aunt and my mom's best friend came, along with her fiancé.

Before the ceremony, a neighbor had helped do my hair. My outfit was thrown together last-minute. I smiled for pictures, but inside, I felt forgotten.

Even in that darkness, something inside me whispered: *You were built for this. You were meant for more than this.* That day, I made a promise to myself:

> *When I grow up, no one will ever hurt me again.*
> *No one will ever make me feel unseen.*
> *I will learn to do my own hair.*
> *I will learn to dress and carry myself with pride.*
> *I will never let anyone shrink me again.*

That whisper became my strength. My flaws weren't curses—they were battle scars. Proof that I, Charmayne, could survive what many people couldn't even imagine.

This was only the beginning of my story—a story full of wounds, tears, abandonment, resentment, and bitterness, but also full of hope. A story carried by a girl who refused to let the darkness she was born into define her.

Chapter 2

Chasing Love in All the Wrong Places

Now that I was a teenager, I thought life would finally get easier. A new journey, new beginnings—boys, high school, and the kind of freedom that's supposed to make everything better.

But what I didn't realize was that I was still carrying the weight of everything that had already happened—the pain, the secrets, and the silence. I carried it quietly, hidden deep inside, because who would listen anyway? No one had ever really shown up for me the way they should have.

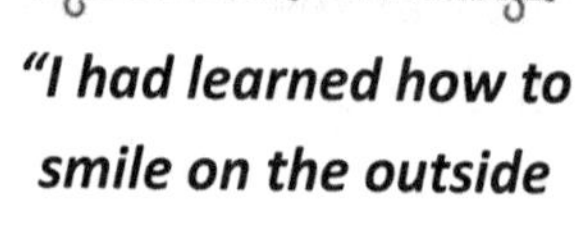

anyway? No one had ever really shown up for me the way they should have.

I had learned how to smile on the outside while breaking on the inside.

In these teenage years, another kind of pain began to take root—one I tried desperately to numb.

At fifteen, I met a boy. He wasn't really a stranger—he was

our neighborhood friend. Before I even turned fifteen, we already thought we were in love. Even when my father tried to keep us apart, we found our ways to be together anyway. Young, wild, and hopeful.

Then I got pregnant.

After that, I got locked up in jail and detention centers because I was reckless. After getting out of jail, I was still pregnant while trying to pick up the pieces of my life. The weight of everything I had been through kept following me.

Before I could even understand what motherhood meant, before I could process that I was bringing a life into this world, it was taken away. I miscarried my baby girl—a tiny life I never got to hold. The pain of that loss was unbearable—but what hurt even more was the confusion that followed. I didn't understand what happened. I didn't know why it happened. I just kept asking, "Why me?"

The thought of loving something or someone, only to lose them, broke something inside of me. I had wanted to care for that baby—maybe because I thought I could finally give someone else the kind of love I had never truly received. Facing that pain alone was devastating.

If I rewind to that time, I can see the beginning of my search—how I had given myself away, believing that love was the price I had to pay to be chosen. I thought sex would make me feel wanted, seen, loved. But it didn't. It left me feeling empty, used, and disgusted with myself. Losing my virginity wasn't what I imagined it to be. It wasn't sacred. It wasn't romantic. It wasn't safe. It was taken from me by someone who wasn't my child's father. Afterward, I carried the weight of that moment everywhere I went. Eventually, I told the guy who would become my boyfriend, and eventually my child's father, what had happened to me.

He didn't leave me after I told him what had happened—he left me after I lost our baby. I became depressed from the grief of losing my child and her father. That's when I began searching for something to ease my mind—something I called attention, something I mistook for love. When people told me I was pretty or looked at me and called me beautiful, I would take it in, thinking it could fill the emptiness I felt inside.

I started believing attention could fill the emptiness I carried. Every "you're pretty" or "you got a nice body" became an invitation to feel something—anything. I told myself I was confident, but the truth was, I was broken. I was looking for someone to fill the emptiness that had

been growing inside me since I was a little girl.
High school only made it worse. I couldn't focus. My
grades slipped. I was always angry, lost, or distracted.
Fights became my outlet—mostly with other girls who
didn't like me because I had been with, or was with, their
boyfriends. I wasn't doing it out of spite. I was doing it
because I believed the lies those boys told. I believed I was
special. I believed I was chosen.

But I wasn't chosen.
I was convenient.
I was new.
I was just someone to make them feel powerful—and I
thought that meant love.

Eventually, after losing my baby, the fights, the
distractions, and the constant feeling of being lost, I
dropped out of school. Staying home, laying up, felt easier
than facing the shame and the judgment that followed me
everywhere I went.

It seemed like everything around me was falling apart—
and no one ever stopped to ask why. Not even me. No one
looked at the patterns. No one saw the broken girl
underneath the behavior. Instead, they judged me. They
called me names. They told me I would never be anything.

"Just like your parents."
"Ain't no good gonna come from you."

"Trash."

And yes—some of those words came from my own family.

Looking back now, I see the truth.
I wasn't fast. I wasn't reckless. I
was hungry. I was looking for love
in every place I had been told it
lived—in attention, in sex, in
being wanted. But every place I
looked turned out to be the
wrong place. Every time I thought
I'd found it, I ended up emptier than before.

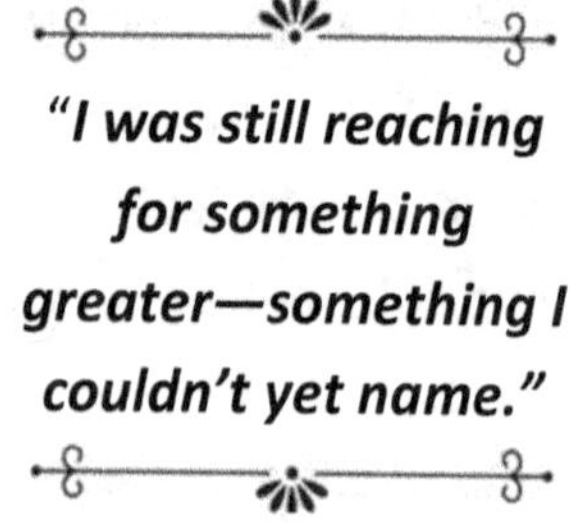

Yet somehow, even in all that brokenness, I survived.

I may have been lost, misguided, and searching, but I was
still reaching for something greater—something I couldn't
yet name. I didn't know it then, but all those wrong places
would eventually lead me to the right one—within myself,
and eventually, to God.

No matter how many times I gave myself away, the love I
was so desperately searching for could never be found in
someone else. It had to begin with me—learning my
worth, my strength, and my truth.

Chapter 3

The Essence of Grace

By the time I turned seventeen, I found myself facing something I never expected—Bell's Palsy. One side of my face became paralyzed, and I had to be hospitalized. I had gone through the same thing at the age of nine, but I didn't know it could happen again. I was scared, confused, and didn't know what was happening. I thank God that my father was sober enough that day, so he and my grandfather were able to come rushing me to the hospital. Without them, I know I would have been completely alone and terrified. As soon as we got to the hospital, the room started spinning. I was throwing up, I felt like I was dying. But deep down, I knew this was not the end of me. After that, I asked myself again, *Why do bad things keep happening to me?*

After recovering, I found myself drawn to the streets. I really had nobody to look after me. My parents were still lost in their own struggles, I was out of foster care, and I considered myself grown. I was homeless, moving between places to sleep wherever I could find a roof over my head. I spent time with my grandmother—my mom's mother—and somehow I ended up dating my grandmother's neighbor. That didn't last long. He was good to me, but I just wasn't satisfied with one person at this point. That's when I started looking for other ways to survive and feel seen and chosen.

I had no accountability. No one checked on me. No curfew. I could do whatever I wanted. Laying up with someone who had a place for me to stay made me feel like I was in control, like I was "that girl"—at least for a moment. I was willing to settle for anything just to feel chosen, yet even in that fleeting sense of belonging, I was still lost.

Then, I met a young woman who would change the course of my life. She didn't just offer me a place to stay; she opened her heart and her home. Maybe she saw something in me that I didn't even see in myself. She had a big heart, was very loving, and knew God. Her house was filled with prayer and worship music, and it felt real—peaceful.

Even as I struggled and made choices that weren't always wise, she never judged me. She introduced me to her sister and her mother, who was a pastor. They eventually became like family to me. When I first arrived at her sister's house, the atmosphere was calm and inviting. Soft gospel music played, the couch was made up with clean sheets, and I felt a heavy burden lift off my shoulders.

We talked, laughed, and shared stories. Eventually, I met her children—my new siblings—and one of them peeked downstairs and said to his mom, "Mom, who's that lady on the couch?" It was a funny moment, but it also marked the beginning of a fresh start for me.

I had heard about God as a child through my father's mother. She was strict and ensured we were in church every Sunday, standing by the mailbox to make sure we walked to Sunday school. But even with all those Sundays sitting in the pews, I never really knew God for myself. To me, He was just a distant figure I had only heard about.

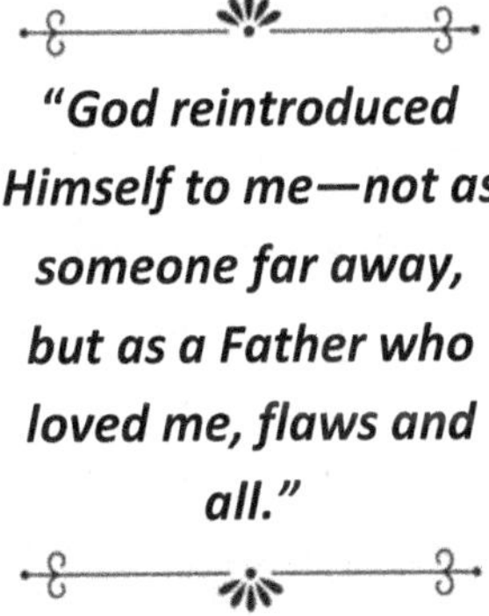

Through this journey, God reintroduced Himself to me— not as someone far away, but as a Father who loved me, flaws and all. The kindness, faith, and unwavering love of my new mom and her mother, who I consider my grandmother, showed me a life I didn't even know I was worthy of. This was my beginning of learning and experiencing Christ.

Looking back now, I see that even in my darkest moments, God had a plan. When I felt forgotten, when I didn't even know who He was, He knew me. He had already prepared people to step into my life. He was always making ways of escape and guiding me back to Him.

When I thought survival was the only way—laying up, searching for men, seeking love in all the wrong places— God found me right where I was. He found me broken, lost, and on the streets. He showed me that I was still His child, and I was still chosen.

Through this, I began to understand that no matter how far I had gone, the love of God was greater than any love I had been searching for. He was writing a new chapter for me—a chapter of healing, guidance, and redemption. Everything God takes you through isn't easy. He takes you through the fire to purify you, and that's exactly what He was preparing to do in my life.

Chapter 4

The Mirror of My Pain

While still living with my adoptive mother, I would never discredit my biological mother. She was still trapped in her own pain. I still loved her. I still thought about her. I even prayed for her because I didn't know what she was really going through. I only judged her. I would say things like, "How can someone love drugs more than they love their own children?" This was my first real lesson that we should never judge something we know nothing about.

When I turned eighteen, guided by my adoptive mother, we went to the welfare office. She helped me apply for assistance and fill out applications to get my own place. The two ladies at the rental office took a liking to me. I don't know what it was, but they pushed everything through for me to get approved. Finally, I had a roof over my head—a place that didn't depend on a man. I had my own freedom, my own space.

"We should never judge something we know nothing about."

I was that type of young woman who didn't like being told

what to do. Having my own place gave me even more leverage to run wild. I did what I wanted, with whomever I wanted. I had friends over, hooking up with guys, throwing parties—I was young, attractive, and felt like I could have anyone I wanted. From the outside, it looked like I had it all together: my hair done, my clothes on point, two jobs, a car. But behind closed doors, I was still broken—sleeping with men I didn't love, waking up empty and disgusted, chasing attention instead of healing.

And slowly, I realized that I was repeating what I once judged my mother for. The chaos, the recklessness, the reliance on men for validation—I was living it all. I was repeating the cycle without even knowing it.

The drama never stopped. Women would show up at my house or blow up my phone, angry and ready to fight over men who had been there with me. I fell back on my pride, ego, and pain. Then, I met a young man—chocolate dark skin, a new face in town. He captured my attention, and I got pregnant with my son. I thought I had found someone who truly wanted my heart, but like so many others before him, he disappeared. How could I blame him? I was wild and reckless. I raised my son by myself.

Even in my recklessness, I found moments of care and protection for others. Three young ladies in my neighborhood drew me in, reminding me of the little girl I used to be. I wanted to be a mother figure, a mentor, a protector—something I never had. I clung to them, even while I was still broken, a single mom living a life full of contradictions.

Then came the dangers I had long feared: I was introduced to drugs by a man who was supposed to be helping me raise my son. He had laced the weed I smoked with cocaine. I didn't know it then. Eventually, he came out and told me what it was, smiling and laughing like it was a joke. What was meant to be "fun" quickly turned into terror. I panicked, my heart raced, my chest hurt. After that, the high came with the same panic attack every time. I swore I would never touch it again, reminding myself of what I had learned from my parents' struggles and my own adolescence: Never go down that path.

For a while, I stayed away. But five years later, I found myself back in it, not because I wanted to, but because that root that was planted started to grow, along with me being weak emotionally and mentally, and life pushing me back into the very thing I swore I would never touch. I didn't know my identity. I didn't know who I was. I clung to these three young ladies and my son as a reminder to not fall, because they needed me, but somehow I felt like I had failed them.

I didn't realize at the time, but these experiences planted a seed that would grow into something darker than I could ever imagine. Now I understand what my parents were going through, because the mirror had now been turned on me.

Chapter 5

East Side Chronicles

As time went by and my son grew older, I wanted something bigger—somewhere my son could have his space, and I could have mine. So, I decided to move into another apartment. These apartments were considered the projects—the same place I grew up in as a child.

It was a place called East Side—familiar, comforting, and complicated. A happy place, but also a heavy place.

It wasn't always bad growing up there. I had some great friends, and we shared beautiful memories together. Those friends became more like family. We laughed, played, and found joy even in the simplest things.

So, returning to East Side as an adult was like stepping back into a place that held both my joy and my pain. I didn't dwell on the brokenness that had happened there; I just wanted something bigger for me and my son. I knew the lady who ran the housing program—she'd known my family for years—and she helped me get my spot.

But what I didn't realize then was that I was bringing my same pain from childhood right back into the same environment—with the same mindset, the same patterns, but I say change isn't good if your mind hasn't been renewed.

Once I moved into the projects, I also tried to be a positive role model for three young girls I had taken under my wing. I poured love and advice into them, telling them to hold their heads high, to carry themselves with self-respect and class, and to choose wisely. But deep down, I knew I hadn't fully learned those lessons myself.

> *"Change isn't good if your mind hasn't been renewed."*

I wasn't walking in my own words.

I was trying to give them what I never received.

Sometimes I did it well, but other times my actions spoke louder than my words. I felt like a hypocrite, battling an identity crisis. The men still came in and out—that was my comfort blanket. I wasn't afraid of the consequences, even when I should have been. I was spreading myself thin, trying to fill a void that couldn't be filled by flesh.

I should've learned when one of my favorite aunts—my mom's sister—passed away from a deadly disease. She was beautiful, admired, and always got attention from men and women. It's crazy, because people just assumed she slept with their men, but come to find out, she never did. She wasn't as promiscuous as people perceived her to be—she was simply beautiful and had her pick of who she wanted. She couldn't help who wanted her.

But behind that beauty was a curse—a generational spirit that had been passed down to me. It followed me, seduced me, and whispered lies to me. Even as I tried to do things my way, I felt a pull toward God.

I started going to church regularly, even while still dancing with the devil.

I was running, hiding, and pretending.

There was a deep ache inside me—shame, guilt, and trauma I never processed. It sat quietly beneath the surface, dormant but alive. I was learning how to smile in public while crying in private. Raising my hands in worship while still living a double life. I was lonely, searching, broken—and trying to heal in all the wrong ways.

By this time, my son was about five or six years old. He was growing up quietly, observing. He kept to himself, but he was collecting every moment—every argument, every stranger that came in and out of the house, every tear I thought he didn't see. He was learning what life looked like through my lens.

That realization hit me hard later—I was repeating the

same cycle I had experienced as a child, only now it was through my son's eyes.

Sheesh.

One night, my best friend (who has now gone on to be with God), my son, and I walked to get something to eat. There was a fish store at the end of Keasbey Street and Broadway. Two guys were working there, and of course, my friend was fast like me. They say birds of a feather flock together—and it was true.

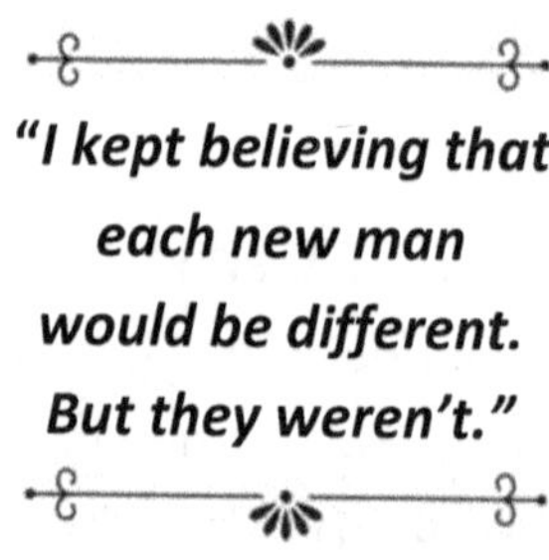

While we ordered our food, one of the guys—the owner's friend—started flirting. He asked what I was doing after he got off work. I told him nothing. My house was just up the street, so it wasn't far. I didn't know then that meeting this man would change everything.

I don't know why I kept thinking a man would change me. I was still young, attractive, and self-absorbed—not in a good way but in a broken way. I used my looks as a mask to hide my pain. I knew I was weak mentally and emotionally, yet I kept believing that each new man would be different. But they weren't.

It wasn't the men—it was the same spirit in different

faces, attaching itself to me, trying to destroy me.

This man, or this demon, said all the right things. He made me feel special. We'd sit outside, laugh, and talk about life. He'd share stories about his children, and I'd talk about mine—my biological son and my three girls. I didn't know God was allowing this for a reason—to teach me, to take me through a journey. This man was part of my test—a test I didn't know was coming. A journey that would shift the entire course of my life.

Not everyone who says they love you really loves you—but I didn't know that yet. I didn't even know what love was. I didn't even know what love *wasn't* either.

As time went by, we got closer. He moved in with me— even though I already had someone else living there. Yes, I'm exposing myself because I have nothing to hide. If my story can help someone else get free, I don't mind getting naked—emotionally, spiritually—and showing my flaws and mistakes.

Nobody really said anything. They knew of each other, but silence sometimes keeps dysfunction alive. I thought I was being the perfect example to my son and my three girls, but truthfully, I wasn't—I was naive and delusional as hell, excuse my language.

Because when you're broken . . .

You can't build anything whole out of the pieces.
And no matter how much love
you try to pour out—
if your cup is cracked, it keeps
leaking.

But even in my brokenness, God
was still watching.
He was still waiting.
He was still whispering, "This is not where your story
ends."

**"Silence sometimes
keeps dysfunction
alive.**

Chapter 6

The Price of Loyalty

After some time, me still living in the projects with this gentleman, Christmas time approached. My son had great Christmases—not because of this gentleman, but because people loved my son so much. He had every toy imaginable: little four-wheelers powered by batteries, and everything a child could dream of. All the little kids in the project wanted to play with him because he had so many nice toys. I threw him the best birthday party; he was obsessed with SpongeBob, so everything was SpongeBob-themed. My son was spoiled, and honestly, he deserved it.

I was working two, sometimes three jobs—one at the hospital, another at my aunt's hair salon on weekends, and another at the movie gallery in the plaza. I had to buy another car because of an accident with my first car—an accident resulting from my poor choices. I had gone to see a guy in jail—the same man I had been with previously, the one who laced the weed with cocaine—along with my ride-or-die best friend, the same young lady who was with me when I met the gentleman I'm talking about now. We thought we were being grown, but somehow I was still making reckless decisions even with a man living in my house.

I thank God that my son wasn't with me that day. I left him with my mom, because at the scene, his car seat was in the front of the dashboard.

The enemy had been trying to take my son from me for the longest. While pregnant, doctors suggested my gallbladder to be removed, yet advised me to abort because the anesthesia would kill the baby. But I declined; I chose to keep my baby. Then, during his birth, things got worse—his heart rate began to drop, and they had to put me to sleep for an emergency C-section. When I woke up, the first thing I did was ask my adopted grandmother what he looked like. She didn't tell me right away that my son had died at birth and had to be brought back to life. The enemy had been trying to get my son since the very beginning, but God said otherwise.

Over time, I began having panic and anxiety attacks so severe that I would just leave work for no reason. I didn't understand what was happening to me. At the same time, things at the housing project started falling apart. I began receiving notices from the housing authority because they considered air conditioners, microwaves, and washers/dryers "miscellaneous items" I had to pay for, even though the development didn't charge for electricity. I ended up getting put out—not for rent, but for not paying these miscellaneous fees. I didn't know I could fight it, and I had no guidance, so I let it go.

I reached out to family. My aunt, who was deep in addiction, told me I could stay with her. I didn't bring my son because I knew her habits would be unsafe for him, so I asked my sister to keep him until I found another place. I still had a job, but I left the hospital and stopped working consistently at my aunt's salon. I got a better job at a school as the site director for an after-school program—more money, more stability.

Living with my aunt was a challenge. Her environment threatened to pull me under. She would let anyone stay as long as they gave her money, but I didn't want to feed into her addiction. So I started selling drugs again to cover my own expenses. I had experience from selling drugs with my previous boyfriend—the same boyfriend who laced the weed with cocaine, the same boyfriend I went to see in jail when I ended up in an accident.

Drugs weren't new to me; I just wasn't experienced enough at it. I was getting the money, I touched the money, I saw the money. I was low-key and careful, keeping my job so no one would suspect. I knew how to move; he taught me well. Again, wanting to be that type of female for a guy—to prove your loyalty—that's who I was, and that's what I did.

It was a Friday night, and I came home from work with drinks—our usual Friday routine—but that night felt different. My aunt asked me for money. She said, "Hey love, do you have any money?" I said, "I don't have any money, but hold on, I'll be right back." As I went upstairs, I asked my boyfriend about the product. He told me where it was, but somehow some of it was missing. I didn't understand. He had this crazy look on his face, and I wondered if he was tricking with my aunt. I paid it no mind because I was feeling good from the drinks, so I gave my aunt what she wanted.

When I came back upstairs, that's when he told me: "I have a confession. The reason the product is missing is because I got high."

I already knew parts of the street life, so I was trying to understand where he was coming from—not knowing I was being manipulated by him so he could get what he wanted. By now, you would think I would have learned to see the tactics of manipulation, but when you're blinded by love—or the *illusion* of love— you don't see anything. And

"I always wanted to be that girl—the loyal one, the one who proved her love."

because I was drinking and feeling good, it was no-holds-barred. He felt like since he made this confession, now he could manipulate me again, this time to get more.

So then he says to me, "If you love me, you would try it."

And because again, I told you I always wanted to be that girl—the loyal one, the one who proved her love—I did it.

That one hit shifted the entire direction of my life. My mind, my emotions, my spirit—all changed in that single moment. The pain I had been running from for years started to surface again.

Trying to love him and being loyal to him made me lose myself all in one night. And I had to ask myself: *What does loyalty mean when it costs you your own soul?*

Chapter 7

All While Chasing Shadows

By this time, the little girl who hated everything about drugs had become the very same thing she once hated. Isn't it ironic how a single moment can change everything? How judging something you know nothing about can suddenly place you right in the middle of it? I had finally felt what it was like to walk in my parents' shoes, especially my mother's—how loving someone and being in love with someone can make you do things that change your life for the rest of your life, all for the sake of being loyal. I had always hated and judged everyone in my family who got high, or even those who sold drugs to my loved ones, but once I did it, I became just like them. The feeling took hold of me like a sudden rush of escape . . . a momentary numb that chased away the pain I didn't know how to face.

I left my aunt's house not because I had to, but because of the sudden urges to get high. I wasn't trying to be complacent with where I was, so I needed to find other avenues, other revenue streams, and other places to feed the habit. I bounced from house to house, body to body, doing whatever I had to just to keep moving, just to keep the feeling alive. I even got high in abandoned buildings, riding with people in cars, driving in my own cars, in the woods, and in the back of churches. Even walking down the street, I would take a hit—anywhere I could feel secluded or just to knock that edge off. Because when the anticipation of wanting that hit and that rush takes over, you don't care where you are, as long as you can satisfy that craving.

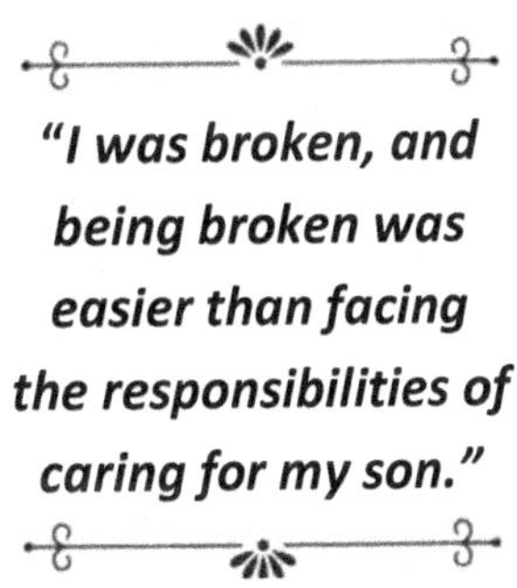

Even while my son was with my sister, I felt this twisted sense of freedom. Not because I didn't love him—I always loved my son, and he was always on my mind. I would check on him to see if he was alright; sometimes I didn't. I loved the high more than I loved myself. I was embarrassed to reach out to him. I gave my son just enough so he wouldn't feel completely abandoned, but I couldn't give him all of me—and that was what he really wanted. I was broken, and being broken was easier than facing the responsibilities of caring for my son.

I didn't feel good about myself anymore. I felt undeserving of anybody's love, not even my son's. I betrayed him and my three "daughters"—three girls of friends of mine who had become like my own children. All the while, they were chasing my love, and I was too far gone, too busy chasing a high. Deep down, I knew I needed God. I knew I needed something to save me before I ended up in total destruction. But at that moment, as a beginner in getting high, nothing else mattered—nobody, not even myself—except that fleeting escape.

Even in the midst of addiction, I still felt God's presence. I would hear church songs, catch a sermon, or hear a word from someone ministering—even from people who themselves were struggling with addiction. One lady, who I was getting high with, told me, "I see something over you. God has a plan for you. You're going to be the one to save us." I didn't pay attention at the time because I was high, chasing my escape.

Even when a drug dealer refused to sell to me because he saw the path I was heading toward—destruction—he looked me straight in the eyes and said, "Either you're going to be for God, or you're going to be for the streets." Then he walked away and didn't sell me anything. That was still God giving me warnings, calling me back, showing me that He can use anyone—anyone at all—to reach you when you're blind to your own danger.

There were nights I stayed up chasing the high, not washing, not brushing my teeth. Yet some days, I could put myself together so well that nobody could tell. I still cried out to God, "Please, Lord, help me. I don't want to live like this. I don't want to die like this." But addiction had such a grip on me that prayer alone couldn't break it. I was torn, tired, too weak to climb out, even when I knew deep down that this life was destroying me.

I was trying to escape my pain, my son was learning to live without my love, and I had no idea where my daughters were. That broke me more than anything, yet it still wasn't enough to make me quit. I became selfish, consumed by my own need for that fleeting high. In that moment, I understood why the Bible warns us not to judge: History was repeating itself. I was the child of addicts, and now my son had become the child of an addict too.

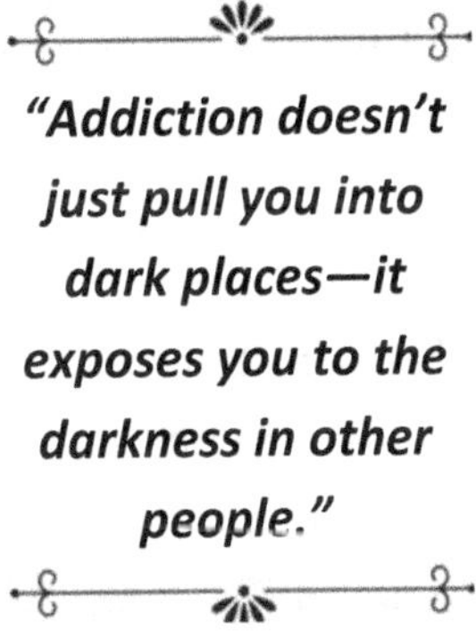

But even in the darkness, there was a glimmer. I knew I couldn't stay there forever. I felt the whisper of hope—that I could rise, that I could reclaim my life, that I could be stronger than the pain and patterns that had plagued my family for generations. I realized that hitting rock bottom didn't have to be the end; it could be the beginning of my freedom, if I had the courage to choose it.

But addiction doesn't just pull you into dark places—it exposes you to the darkness in other people. One day, after one of my aunts passed away, my uncle asked me to go to her house with him. I thought we were going there to grieve or to pick up something for the family, but I didn't know he had a different plan. He took me there so he and my aunt's boyfriend could get me high and then try to sleep with me. They thought my addiction made me accessible, easy, willing—like I had no lines and no worth left.

But even in the middle of that life, even when I was at my weakest, I thank God I still had some dignity left inside me. Some boundary that couldn't be crossed. I didn't care what people said about me, what they thought they knew about me, or how deep into addiction I had fallen—there were certain things I was not going to allow. I snapped on them both and walked away. Because even an addict has limits. Even a broken woman still has a voice. And in that moment, I knew this was a wicked game.

Because the thing about brokenness is this: You can feel lost, enslaved, trapped, and still, the possibility of healing is always there. Even when you're chasing shadows, even when the night seems endless, the dawn can come. And when it does, you can step into the light of your own redemption, piece by piece, one choice at a time.

Chapter 8

Love in Its Purest Form

My son, Cyn'cere—he is exactly what his name means—has always had a heart bigger than his years. Even when life didn't give him everything he needed, he somehow found ways to give to others. I'll never forget one Christmas. While living with my sister and attending a school program where children received gifts, Cyn'cere received a brand-new pair of sneakers—just for him.

But instead of keeping them for himself, he looked around, saw a classmate in need, and without hesitation, gave his sneakers away. At the time, I didn't even know what he had done. When I asked him where his shoes were, he didn't answer. Later, I learned he didn't tell me because he didn't want his friend to feel embarrassed. That's the heart of Cyn'cere: quiet, giving, protective, and respectful. Even as I was lost in my own struggles, he was out here giving love and compassion—freely and without expectation.

Cyn'cere discovered his passion in basketball. He had talent, discipline, and determination, but I wasn't always there to witness it. So many games, so many moments, I missed while chasing highs and trying to numb my own guilt. Yet when I did manage to make it to his games, his face would light up like I was the only person in the world who mattered. In that moment, I realized he wasn't thinking about all the times I wasn't there—he was just grateful I finally showed up.

It broke me. I had always felt undeserving of love, but here was my son, showing me unconditional love despite my failures. He gave me grace when I thought I couldn't be forgiven. He gave me presence when I couldn't give it to him. And somehow, he did it all with a smile.

I also realized that God had placed a strong village around him—my sisters, brothers, cousins, even the teachers and daycare staff. They were there for him when I wasn't. They celebrated his victories, attended his games, and cheered him on. They lifted him up in ways I couldn't. And through all of this, my son continued to shine, showing me that love, consistency, and support matter deeply—but even in their absence, resilience and compassion can thrive.

There are lessons in Cyn'cere's life that I want everyone to see:

- Love isn't measured by perfection. Even broken, I was able to receive his love, and he was able to give it despite my mistakes.

- Giving to others is a gift. Even small acts of kindness, like giving someone your sneakers, can leave a lasting impact. Presence matters more than perfection. Showing up, even when you're not perfect, matters more than all the times you fail.

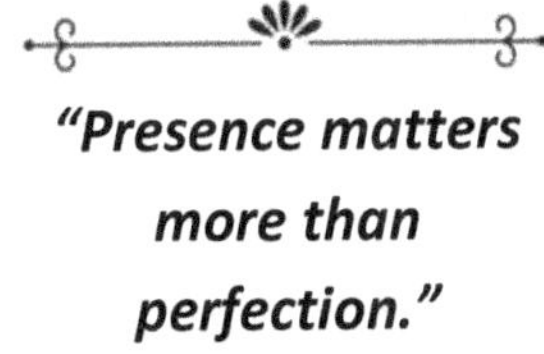

- Community strengthens a child. If you can't be there in every moment, surrounding them with supportive people can help fill those gaps.

Cyn'cere gave what I couldn't: love, sacrifice, compassion, and presence. And through him, I learned that no matter how lost we may be, no matter how broken, God can still use us to raise children who are full of light. I thank God every day for a son like him, who reminds me that even in my darkest moments, love can shine brighter than our failures.

Cyn'cere continues to inspire me, and I hope his story inspires others: Your children may be stronger than you realize, and even in your imperfections, they can teach you lessons you never thought you'd learn.

Deliverance in the Midst of Chaos

After moving from house to house, sometimes staying at my sister's just to be with my son, we finally left. We finally got another place. On the surface, it looked like I was putting my life together again, reclaiming my dignity. But truthfully, I was still reckless. I was still chasing the same old lifestyle, the same emotions, and the same habits that had once consumed me. Moving to a new location didn't change the path I was on—it only gave me a new stage to perform my old ways.

By the time I had moved to Penns Grove, I would return sometimes to my hometown, Salem. I went with a purpose—familiar streets, familiar faces, familiar ways to get what I wanted. I knew how to navigate the places and the people, how to hustle, manipulate, and bend situations to my advantage. I knew exactly how to scheme, flirt with my eyes, and get what I wanted without anyone realizing my intent.

That's when I met another man . . . and let me tell you, when will I ever learn? What was I looking for this time? Another opportunity to complicate my life, another person to charm, another mess to accidentally step into? Yes, I met another man—still searching, still scheming, still somehow thinking I could get it all right this time.

At first, I saw him as just another person I could manipulate, just another situation I could turn to my advantage. I knew the tricks, the tears, the stories—all the ways an addict and a schemer like me could get what I wanted. But this man wasn't buying it. He had a way about him, a quiet strength, a connection to God that I couldn't twist or control.

And what I didn't see coming was that God was already at work. What the enemy intended for harm, God was turning for good. This man became the doorway to a ministry that would change the course of my life and add to my next journey.

I became a part of that ministry, initially wearing deceit like armor. I smiled, sat in the right places, nodded at the right moments—pretending I was healed, delivered, and set free. On the surface, I looked like I had it all together. Behind closed doors, though, I was still chasing highs, still hiding from my pain, still wrestling with my addiction and my past.

This ministry was strict, more disciplined than anything I'd ever experienced. But through its challenges, I learned lessons I could never have gotten anywhere else. I cannot discredit the growth that came from that time—even the hard, uncomfortable, and sometimes humiliating moments.

I wore deliverance like a disguise. I dressed the part—heels, suits, the "first lady" walk, hair done, etc. In the meantime, I started going to adult day classes to get my GED through social services. In order to receive full benefits, I had to take a class. I graduated at the age of thirty. So no matter how old you are, it's never too late to go back and get done what needs to be done. It's never too late to keep working on you. He even sat in class with me! I thought he was there guiding me the whole time, but he was really there watching me! Even when I would resist at times, he stayed there, making sure I didn't wander off my path. He also encouraged me to take care of myself, helping with dentist appointments and making sure I was doing what I needed to grow, even when I pushed back.

After getting my GED, I went to hair school chasing my passion because making people feel beautiful was always my dream—only to be told I had to pause because I wasn't fully delivered from my past. That crushed me. That's when anger set in, along with facing church hurt, rejection, and judgment from those who were supposed to love and uplift me. When I tried to share my struggles honestly, I was dismissed or looked down upon.

Because of that—having to leave my career and still being

in the ministry, feeling dismissed and looked down upon—
I ran back to addiction. I became defiant. I went back to
my old ways, and I was back to feeling the pain of not
feeling accepted. I broke out the church van windows and
kicked in the door. Along with fighting in the ministry, I
became a person I didn't even know. Police were called,
restraining orders were filed. But God never left me, never
stopped shaping me.

Even after all that—the hurt, being reckless, angry, in and
out of court—I finally decided to leave that ministry. My
adoptive family came and got me. They opened their
doors back to me, along with their hearts. My grandfather,
who never sugarcoated anything, said to me, "Charmayne,
how can someone so beautiful be so stupid?" I couldn't
say anything because he was right. He also said to me,
"Charmayne, it's not as hard as you make it. Once you
surrender to God, everything will work out." On his
deathbed, as I sat next to him, I asked, "Poppop, are you
mad at me?" He said, "No. It's not my place. Just give it to
God and let Him handle the rest." And in that moment, I
realized that surrender isn't weakness—it's power. Giving
it all to God opens doors to freedom, restoration, and the
life you were meant to live. It reminded me that even
when life is messy, even when we fall, faith and surrender
are stronger than fear.

Through all this, my mother was being transformed as
well. The same ministry that challenged me became the

vessel through which God began to heal her. Today, she stands fifteen years clean—set free, delivered, and restored. I give God all the glory for that miracle!

And it was in that moment I finally understood: God knew my heart. God knew my intent. God saw all my pain saw all my pain, all my mistakes, all my brokenness, and still He said, "Bring it all to Me."

So, I did. I brought every broken piece, every disappointment, every demon, every high, every tear, every fear—every part of myself that I thought was lost—to Him. And in that surrender, He began to redeem what the enemy had tried to destroy.

> *"God saw all my pain saw all my pain, all my mistakes, all my brokenness, and still He said, 'Bring it all to Me.'"*

I learned that true deliverance isn't about perfection. It's about transparency, humility, and persistence. It's about showing up for God, even when you're messy, flawed, and human. God doesn't need my performance, my schemes, or my tricks. He only needs my heart—broken, honest, and willing.

And that is when my story began to change. I was no longer just running, hiding, or performing. I was *becoming*—the woman God created me to be, the woman who could rise through her pain, the woman whose gift could no longer be stolen or manipulated by anyone.

Even in my chaos, even in my mistakes, God had a plan. And He is still writing it—beautiful, redemptive, and unstoppable. But that didn't mean it was going to be easy. I still had to go through a journey, and every step, every challenge, every tear was part of becoming who I was meant to be.

High Stakes, Empty Tanks

Being back at my adopted grandparents' house, I started having terrible panic and anxiety attacks again—but this time, they seemed worse. I didn't know where they came from, but they began to control my life. I started losing a lot of weight because I was scared to eat. Even going to church or being around too many people triggered me. I think I had been hurt, broken, and disappointed so much that being around people made me panic.

It got so bad that sometimes I would pass out in the middle of church or in public. No matter where I was or what I was doing, those panic attacks would come out of nowhere and take me down.

While living with my grandmother, she became the director of a program and helped me get into another apartment. You see how God keeps showing up? Even in my mess, He was still working things out for me. I wasn't delivered from drugs yet—honestly, I don't think I was ready to let them go. But even in my addiction, even when I wasn't ready to change, God kept opening doors for me. Now I understand that every open door was leading me closer to where He wanted me to be.

I got approved for a new house—one that a relative owned—and by February of 2017 or 2018, me and my son had a fresh start again. He never showed disappointment,

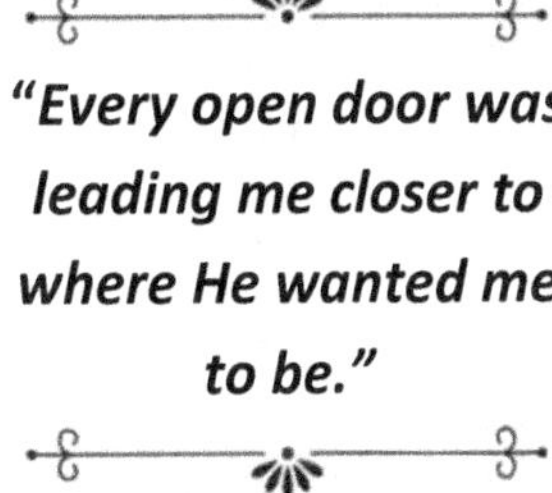

"Every open door was leading me closer to where He wanted me to be."

no matter how many times we had to move because of my dysfunction. We picked our rooms, got cable and an alarm system, and for a brief moment, it looked like we were going to be okay.

But I was too deep in addiction. Every house I got eventually became a trap house—a place for getting high, not healing. My son was happy just to have a home, but I turned it into darkness. That boy has always been one of the most humble souls I've ever known—not just because he's my son, but because anyone who meets him says the same thing.

One day, I was sitting on the front porch of my new house and saw someone I knew from childhood riding by on a bike. He was older than me, but familiar. He stopped, we talked, he was heading to the liquor store, and asked if I wanted something to drink. I said yes—and you already know what happened next.

I didn't know it then, but I had just met another addiction—this time, in human form. The first time we got high, we were intimate. Then he moved in. He became my "get high" partner. We got high together, sold things together, slept together, made promises and broke them all in the same breath.

Truth was, I didn't love him. I didn't even know what love was. I kept him around because I didn't want to be alone. I was desperate for attention, for someone to fill the emptiness inside me. If he wanted me, I stayed. I sold my body just to get high. We'd go do odd jobs together, sometimes just to have money for drugs. I even let him sleep with other women in front of me—just so he wouldn't leave. That's how broken I was.

Men who get high have a hunger that's never satisfied— for the drug, for women, for control. And if you think drug dealers are different, think again. Many of them have been with the same people they sell to. I'm proof.

At one point, I ended up in the hospital. Of course, he showed up there with something for me. Nothing else mattered anymore—not my son, not my health, not myself. I convinced myself it was love, but deep down, I knew it was self-destruction. After that, I signed myself out of the hospital and went right back into the chaos I had created.

My home was full of drugs and roaches, broken promises, and ugly, loud laughter that the whole town gossiped about. The dishes stayed dirty, the lights were off half the time, and I neglected the one person who needed me most—my son.

He started to change before my eyes. He wasn't the same happy boy anymore. He was angry, distant, hanging with the wrong crowd, smoking weed, talking back, leaving the house without telling me. I couldn't even blame him. He had watched his mother fall apart for years—crying, getting high, being abused, and giving herself away to men and to drugs.

He once even found a drug bag in the bathroom and never told me. I later found out. My son had seen too much. He even watched me stay with the same man he once tried to help fight off me.

By then, I was numb—not just from the drugs, but from life itself. I didn't care about bills, food, love, or even myself. I was just a shell walking around pretending to be alive. Every day I found myself selling my son's things, selling food stamps, selling anything just to get high.

His breaking point came when someone blessed him with something, and later that day, he saw one of my drug dealers wearing what used to belong to him. That broke him. That was the moment I think he lost the last bit of faith he had in me.

Eventually, my reckless lifestyle caught up with me. One

night I was drinking at my house, and the police showed up. I was arrested for credit card fraud. I was good with numbers—I could memorize them easily—and started stealing card numbers, scamming people for money, even pretending to be stranded with a gas can just to get cash. I wore scrubs and told people I was a nurse whose car ran out of gas—and they believed me.

I was a mess. I got in cars with strangers, met men on dating apps, told them it was my birthday every day just to get money for drugs. I even ended up stranded at a stranger's house once—my sister and brother-in-law had to come rescue me. Anything could have happened—I could've been raped, killed, or worse. But the truth is, at that point, I didn't care. I didn't care about anything.

Chapter 11

Addicted to Chaos

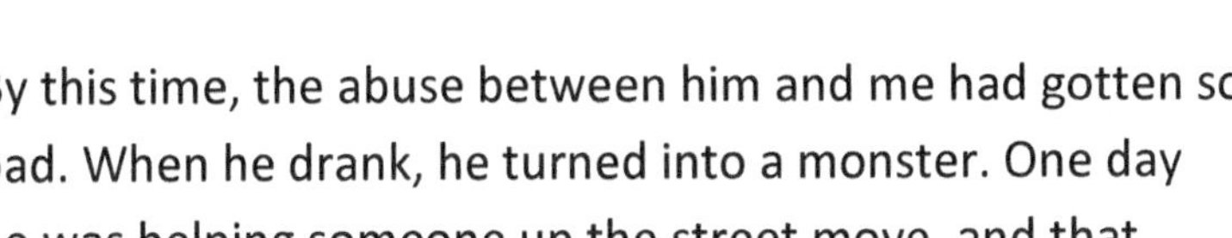

By this time, the abuse between him and me had gotten so bad. When he drank, he turned into a monster. One day he was helping someone up the street move, and that person gave him three of the biggest bottles of vodka I had ever seen. I don't even remember the brand, but I remember the chaos that followed.

While he was out, I was home. The very thing we had done together—sleeping with other people—he thought I was doing while he was gone. When he came in and found me in the bathroom, he snapped. He beat me so bad that my head had lumps, my eye was swollen shut, and my lip was busted. I didn't think I was going to make it out alive that night.

All those times my brother wanted to beat him up, my father wanted to destroy him—I never let them. I kept saying, "I love him." Even when my son tried to protect me, I still stayed. I stayed when he locked me in an abandoned house with him. My brothers and my son had to come and rescue me, and after all that . . . I went right back to him.

Even after he filed restraining orders on me because I started fighting back, I still brought him back into my life. But that last night—when he beat me until I was unrecognizable—that was the breaking point. When I finally broke free, I ran across the street to the neighbor's house, covered in blood and fear. It took everything in me to want to stay free this time.

I called the police because deep down, I knew if I didn't, I might not live to see another day. As they put him in the cop car and drove away, I felt both terrified and relieved. I went to the station, filed the report, and then went to my mom's house with my son because I was afraid to go back home that night—I didn't know if he would come back out.

Here's the thing about me: I've always been weak and vulnerable when it comes to attention. Anytime someone shows me care, concern, or affection, I fall for it. This time, it wasn't a man—it was a woman.

After leaving my mom's house, I met this individual who came into my life when I was completely shattered— scared, broken, but still breathing. At first, we would just talk. Simple, friendly conversations that made me feel human again. I put on my mask, pretending to be clean, pretending I wasn't getting high anymore. When you meet new people, you try to present your best self, hiding the broken pieces until they start to show.

This individual made me feel seen—like I mattered. They helped me rearrange my home, make it feel alive again. I even started to take care of myself: getting my hair done, looking in the mirror without shame. I wasn't getting high at that moment, though truthfully, I was only masking it. I still wasn't ready to let it go completely.

Still, I started to live again. This individual helped me find a job. I was working, trying to build some kind of normal life. It felt like life was finally giving me and my son a break.

But the streets—they have a way of reminding you who they think you are. The truth is, I wasn't done with them, and they weren't done with me.

One night, there was a shootout. My house was shot up—on my son's birthday, January 2. It was like a nightmare I couldn't wake up from. Bullets flying, fear gripping my chest so tight I couldn't breathe. My son and I hit the ground, praying we'd survive. My heart pounded so hard it felt like it was going to break through my chest.

That same individual stayed calm and called the police. After the investigation, they helped put us up in a hotel, thinking it would be for just a night or two. But those nights turned into weeks, and those weeks became our new reality. That hotel became our home—not because we wanted it to, but because we had no other choice.

Even in that small room, I told myself, *I'm not going back. Not this time. Not with my son here. I want him to see me trying.*

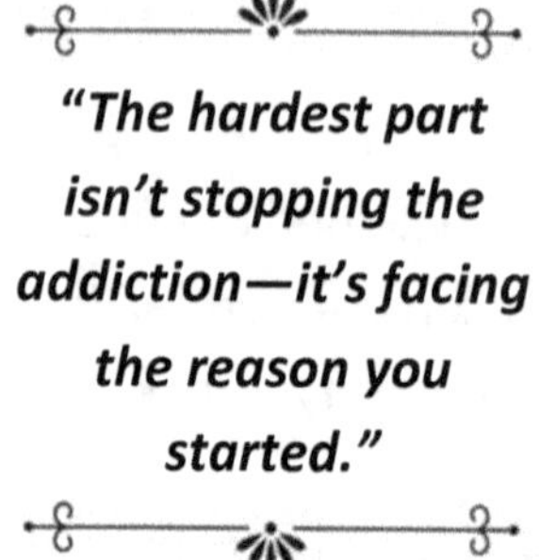

"The hardest part isn't stopping the addiction—it's facing the reason you started."

At this point, you may be reading this rollercoaster story and wondering, *When is she going to turn things around—for good this time?* I get it . . . the up-and-down lifestyle, the chaos . . . but one thing was constant: God *never* gave up on me, no matter the number of chances I was given. He had a better plan for my life.

But here's the truth—because I hadn't faced my demons or healed from the inside, the cravings never left. The pain never left. I was still masking my hurt, and the things we bury always find a way to resurface.

You can only pretend for so long before the truth catches up. The hardest part isn't stopping the addiction—it's facing the reason you started.

The Price of Comfort

Even though I had been in same-sex relationships before, my first experience with a woman was back in 2015. That relationship offered me and my son comfort, stability, and a kind of love that felt different from anything I had known before. The truth is, that individual was good to me— better than I was to myself. They gave me consistency, care, and support at a time when my life felt uncertain.

But I wasn't in a healthy place then. The version of me they got was still broken, still lost, still searching for something I couldn't even name. I lied. I stole. I betrayed their trust. And even though that chapter ended years ago, I still carry the regret and shame of how I hurt someone who didn't deserve it. However, I'll always carry respect for what we shared and gratitude for the lessons it taught me—lessons that would later come back around in ways I never expected.

Years later, I found myself in another same-sex relationship—one that looked different on the outside but came with its own kind of lessons. It wasn't all bad; there were good moments too. With this individual, I wanted for nothing. We had good holidays, thoughtful birthdays, nice dinners, and memorable trips. I'll never take that away from them. They showed up for me and my son in ways that, for a time, made us feel secure. But as I've learned, even comfort comes with a price.

In earlier chapters, I talked about how I used to judge my mother for some of her choices, especially around relationships and identity. But life has a way of humbling you. It's almost as if God allowed me to walk some of the same paths she did—even with who I chose to love—so I could understand rather than criticize.

That relationship gave me and my son what we thought we needed: stability, affection, and a sense of belonging. I'll be honest—I was drawn to people who seemed to have it together financially. It wasn't that I didn't contribute or bring anything to the table—I worked hard, held multiple jobs, and gave from my heart—but deep down, I craved the kind of safety that money and consistency seemed to promise.

Looking back, I see how much of that came from my need to please people. I've always been a giver, sometimes to my own detriment. Even in my lowest moments, when addiction still had a grip on me, I shared what little I had. It's who I was—generous, but also searching for acceptance.

That relationship offered comfort, but I started to notice

the cost. What began as protection slowly turned into control. What once felt like strength started to feel like dominance. I found myself shrinking again—bending, adapting, and walking on eggshells just to keep the peace. From the outside, everything looked fine: a new home, my son with me, a partner by my side. But beneath the surface, the energy was unpredictable and heavy.

And if I'm being honest, I still wasn't free from my addiction. That alone made everything harder. I can't put all the blame on anyone else because when you're fighting internal battles, it's easy to find yourself in unhealthy situations. I was vulnerable, tired, and spiritually drained.

Eventually, things fell apart. I lost my home and found myself in conflict that led to separation and distance. There were tense moments, hard words, and painful choices. It was a breaking point that forced me to face myself again.

"Just because something feels different doesn't mean it's healthy."

Still, I don't believe anything was truly taken from me. What's meant for me will always find its way back in God's timing. Losing that space wasn't punishment—it was protection. It was God's way of clearing the path for something better.

What I learned from that chapter of my life is simple but powerful: Just because something feels different doesn't mean it's healthy, and just because someone challenges you doesn't always mean they're helping you grow. Sometimes, you can't step into the promised land while still dragging pieces of your past with you.

Chapter 13

The Moment My Soul Cried Out

As me and this individual were in the process of calling it quits, we said it was mutual—but honestly, it wasn't. Things had happened that left me with no other choice but to walk away.

During that time, I was still battling my addiction. It had gotten so bad that even the anticipation of getting high would send my body into chaos. The moment I knew I had money and was about to pick up, my body reacted before I even touched anything—I would lose control of my bowels. I know that sounds raw, but I promised myself I'd tell the truth in this book, no matter how ugly it looked. That's how deep it had me—it didn't just control my mind; it controlled my body too.

If you've ever been there, you know what I mean. You can go all day without using the bathroom, but the second you know you're about to get high, it's like every part of your body starts reacting at once. That's how far gone I was.

Around that time, I ran into a long-time friend—someone I'd known since I was thirteen. He was a year younger, but he'd always carried wisdom beyond his years. He never judged me. We'd sit outside for hours, just talking about life. He listened, he encouraged, and he reminded me of who I used to be.

This was during the COVID period, when I was living off unemployment. People were losing jobs left and right, but he told me something that stuck with me. He said, "No matter what you're doing in life, no matter how bad it looks—get yourself something that's yours. Something nobody can take from you."

When that next unemployment payment hit, his words kept ringing in my ear. So I decided to do it—I went to a car dealership and bought myself another car. That moment was huge for me. It wasn't just about transportation. It was about taking a piece of my life back. For once, I had something that was mine. Paid off, in my name. And for the first time in a long time, I felt hope.

After dropping my son off at my adoptive sister's house, I went back to my old patterns. I had to drop him off there because the house we had been living in during my last relationship wasn't a place he felt safe or comfortable anymore. He didn't want to be there; he felt disrespected, and I had to respect that. That decision was hard, but necessary for his well-being.

Even with that step to protect him, I repeated the same

destructive cycle. I went to my usual spot to get high. I didn't like crowds or noise when I got high—I needed a space that felt safe, quiet, controlled. I smoked and drank, and I also added weed to help mellow everything out so I wouldn't be chasing the high. Over time, I started learning new ways to manage the addiction in those moments, or at least how to navigate it without completely losing myself.

I was a friendly drunk during those times—I would buy everything I needed, from the drugs to the drinks, wherever I went. It became a ritual of sorts, a combination of familiarity, control, and escape, even though I knew it wasn't truly controlling anything.

But something different happened that night. I started crying—out of nowhere. At first, I thought it was the high, or maybe the alcohol. But it wasn't. This time felt different. This wasn't just my emotions talking. It was my soul crying out.

I didn't say some polished church prayer. I prayed the realest prayer I ever prayed in my life. Pipe in one hand, tears in my eyes, I said:

"God, I'm tired.
I need Your help.
If You don't do this for me, it won't get done.
Because truth is—I enjoy this too much. I love the

numbness, the rush, the escape.
But I'm tired of disrespecting myself.
I'm tired of hurting my son.
I'm tired of hurting You.
God, I'm scared.
If You don't get me out of this, I'm going to die in it.
Do it for me, Lord. Please."

In that moment, something shifted—not instantly, but definitely. I didn't stay in that house. When I got up, the individual whose house it was asked me, "Are you okay? Is everything okay? What's wrong?" I said, "I love you," and left. That prayer might not have sounded holy, but it was honest—and that honesty made it holy enough for

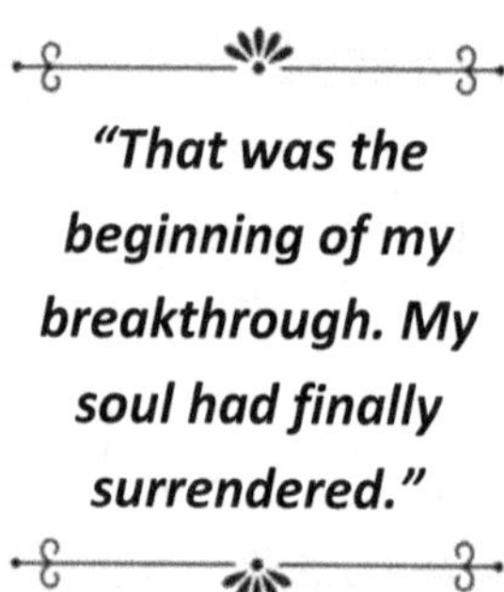

"That was the beginning of my breakthrough. My soul had finally surrendered."

God to hear and to touch His heart, because He knew it came straight from mine.

I didn't realize it then, but that was the beginning of my breakthrough. My soul had finally surrendered.
My mind was tired. My heart was tired. My spirit was tired. And for the first time, I really meant it.

When I walked out of that house, I felt lighter. The weight I had carried for years started to lift. That was the day I knew—freedom had found me.

I didn't walk out of that house as a changed woman that night—but I walked out as a willing one. And that's all God needed. My "yes" in that moment became the start of my healing. From that day forward, I began to believe that no matter how broken I felt, I could reclaim my life. That night marked the first real step toward freedom—and I knew I would never go back.

Chapter 14

December 4, 2020—The Day of Redemption

December 4, 2020—the day I woke up after a night of praying and crying out to God. Normally, waking up meant cravings, withdrawals, and the desperate urge to find money just to get high again. My body was so used to the high that without it, I felt sick, exhausted, sweating

repetitively, in pain, empty, and lost. For those who haven't experienced it, withdrawal is what happens when your body is used to a substance and can no longer get it—your body and mind go into distress, causing physical pain, emotional turmoil, and a desperate need to feel normal again.

But that morning, something was different. No cravings. No urges. No withdrawals. I woke up free.

In that moment, I knew God had heard my prayers. He had seen the intent of my heart. People may judge by the outside, but God sees the heart. He knows when we're ready and when we're not. At any given moment, He knows that if He gives us something too soon and we're not ready for it, we may destroy it—or if He gives us something when we're not ready, it may somehow find a way to destroy us as well. Growth doesn't always happen in the destination; it happens in the journey. God allows us to go through certain things not to hurt us, but to help us. His timing is always perfect, and His strength is made perfect in our weakness.

This is why we have to be patient. And if you know someone who is struggling, please don't be impatient with them. Maybe they're not ready yet, and that's okay—they'll know when they are. Just like when you're ready to let go of a relationship, or finally break free from an addiction, you'll know when it's time.

The weight that had been crushing me lifted. I didn't need to fix anything. I didn't need to get high. I wasn't running anymore—I wasn't scared to answer phone calls because I owed people money. I wasn't running from addiction, from people, or from myself. I was moving toward freedom. Sobriety had truly begun, not as a goal but as a reality I could feel in my bones.

By this time, my son and I were living with my grandmother, but space was tight. Most of our belongings were packed in our car, and some days it felt like we were living out of it. Most days, we did live out of our car. I didn't want my son to live like that. When I got money for a hotel, I packed our essentials and moved us out. My son needed safety and stability—and I wasn't willing to compromise that.

Even in these struggles, he stepped up. At just the right age, he got his first job—and it wasn't an easy job. He was moving carts from the parking lot into the store, a physically tiresome task. Yet he did it while still dealing with homelessness, getting up for school, going to football practices, and playing in football games. He never missed a day of work, never missed school, and never missed a practice during that challenging time. Not too many people knew what we were going through, but his close friends did.

Even though he carried anger and frustration built up from when I was in my addiction phase, he never judged me. He pushed that aside, acting as if nothing ever happened. He was my strength when I needed it most—a constant reminder of the resilience I didn't know I still had. That's what forgiveness was—because he saw me trying. That's why I believe he pushed it aside. Not saying that it was fully dealt with, just that it wasn't brought up; he never talked about it.

Some of you might wonder why I wasn't working at that time. Mentally, I couldn't handle a lot of things. If you've never been in a similar situation, it is hard to imagine what this is like. Drugs can have an effect on your mental health, along with trauma and abuse—mental, physical, and spiritual. Those battles don't just bruise the body; they drain the mind and soul.

Some people can work and have an addiction, some can't. Some people are functional addicts—able to maintain work, relationships, and responsibilities while using. Some people are dysfunctional addicts—they can't maintain jobs or responsibilities because the addiction controls their life. I fell into the dysfunctional addict category.

But even through all that, I used my unemployment responsibly—paying for essentials, hotel stays, and leaning on a support program that helps people leaving abusive situations.

To stay on track, I enrolled in an outpatient program—not because anyone forced me, but because I was ready. I was done with chaos, done with losing, done with hurting myself. I needed something to anchor me to sobriety.

And that's when the blessings started showing up, one by one. God aligned everything. My outpatient counselor became a guiding voice, seeing potential in me that I couldn't see in myself. She didn't sugarcoat anything. She said, "If you don't want it, I don't want it. You've got to want it more than I do. Stay clean." After that, I was about a few months clean and fully committed to my sobriety. She

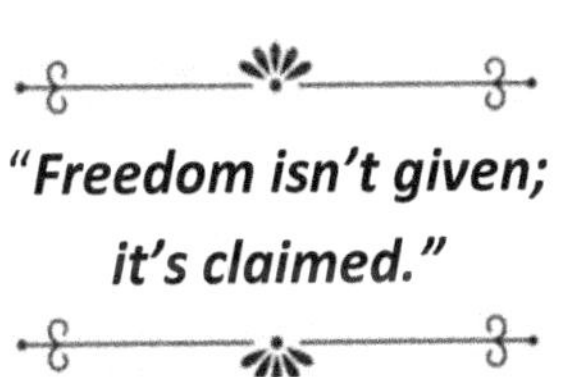

"Freedom isn't given; it's claimed."

was firm, sincere, and persistent, and she already saw the winner in me—long before I did.

Everything in my life may not have been fixed, but I finally knew I had the strength to face it all—without running, without numbing, without manipulating situations, without hiding. I realized freedom isn't given; it's claimed. And in that moment, I claimed mine—my son, my life, my soul. I could finally fight for all of it, and nothing could take that away from me but God.

Chapter 15

I'm No Longer Your Favorite Version

Even though I was still actively attending outpatient recovery and fighting every day to stay sober and clean, life didn't stop testing me. We were still living in that hotel, and the outpatient meetings were held on Zoom because of COVID. The only time we were allowed in the building was for random urine tests. I was consistent with the Zoom calls, even though at first I was slacking. But I was determined to get back on track. Somehow, no matter how hard it was, I made every meeting.

No matter how hard we tried to stay ahead, the bills eventually caught up. If anyone has ever had to stay in a hotel long-term, you know how fast that money adds up. Even if you're only paying for the room, it becomes overwhelming. And to make matters worse, when I started slipping on payments, one of the hotel managers began neglecting the AC. My son and I were melting in the heat, buying fans just to survive the nights. It got creepy to the point where this individual would sit outside our room across the area, pretending to garden, but really watching us. That was my sign—it was time to leave.

With no other option, we put what little we had in storage and went back to my adopted grandmother's home. It was unexpected, but what else could I do? I was still determined to stay sober, and the enemy sure had a way of testing me. But through it all, I never once thought about going back to the streets. My mind was made up, my heart was determined to stay clean.

Not long after settling with my adopted grandmother, I landed a job as a canvasser for the government of New Jersey. I was hired on a Monday, and by Wednesday, I was promoted to supervisor. It happened so fast, I knew it was nothing but God showing me that when one door closes, another opens.

Of course, not everyone understood or was happy about my success. Some people I hoped would be proud of me questioned how I got the promotion. One individual even had the nerve to ask, "Charmayne, what did you have to do to get that position?" Y'all know me—I wanted to knock that person out! But I didn't. I laughed instead, because my past didn't make me unworthy of

"Some people don't want to see you grow. They like you at the version of yourself they can manipulate or frown upon. Once they see you excel, it makes their demons uncomfortable, because they want to keep you at the level they choose for you."

progress. Maybe some people would always remember me for my struggles, or maybe they just couldn't handle the new me. But I had nothing to prove—because sometimes, some people don't want to see you grow. They like you at the version of yourself they can manipulate or frown upon. Once they see you excel, it makes their demons uncomfortable, because they want to keep you at the level they choose for you.

I worked hard at that new job. I met amazing people and tried to give everyone an opportunity, regardless of who they were. I wanted to see people succeed. That's who I am—a giver, a helper. Even to this day, people I worked with tell me how much of a positive difference I made as a supervisor, how I turned a physically demanding job into something exciting, something they looked forward to. I knew God was guiding my efforts, blessing my work. Being a supervisor wasn't new to me—addiction had just gotten in the way before.

One day, I got a phone call from a landlord about an apartment I knew nothing about. My counselor had mentioned she might be moving out, but she didn't tell me anything further. When I arrived, the lease was already printed with my and my son's names, and the keys were waiting. There was no first month's rent required, and the landlord didn't even ask for a security deposit. We asked him how much the security deposit would normally be, and he told us. My biological mother said we should give him something anyway—not because he asked, but because it felt right. We didn't have the money on hand, so my biological grandmother went to the bank to get the funds for the deposit. We didn't even have to give half; he said we could just give something if we chose to. That's what we did. Of course, I worked hard to pay my grandmother back, and I earned every penny—and I didn't have to compromise myself in any way. When God gives you favor, it often arrives wrapped in ordinary moments— a key in hand, a lease with your name on it, people who show up for you when you need them most.

We went straight to cleaning the apartment. My biological mom and I love cleaning, so we went all out, even though it wasn't in perfect shape. Mind you, my counselor had just moved out, and I didn't know it was her until later when she told me. I even hired a contractor to repaint the walls and a cleaning company to steam-clean the carpets throughout the whole apartment. When I say I didn't care how much it cost, I didn't—because this was something worth investing in. This wasn't just a place to live; it was a fresh start, a home that reflected my hard work, my determination, and the favor God had shown me.

Later, my counselor told me she hadn't said anything

about the apartment because she wanted me to work for it, to be accountable and responsible—and that's exactly what I did. I finally graduated from the outpatient program. Every challenge, every struggle I had faced up to that point—the homelessness, the hotel stays, the uncertainty—had led me here. I had stayed accountable, stayed sober, and stayed determined, and God's favor had placed me in this moment.

Toward the last day of my outpatient program, a friend I had grown close to called me. They shared that my Zoom counselor, who I had grown to inspire, spoke about me as someone who had become a light for them. They said my journey showed that no matter what life throws at you, it's possible to stay clean and focused. Even through homelessness, hotels, uncertainty, and moving from place to place, I had stayed consistent, resilient, and focused on what mattered.

That moment reminded me that God can use your journey—every struggle, every test—to encourage and uplift others. Every challenge, every hardship, every test I faced was not in vain. God's favor finds you, lifts you, and uses your story—even when the world doubts you—to inspire someone else to keep going.

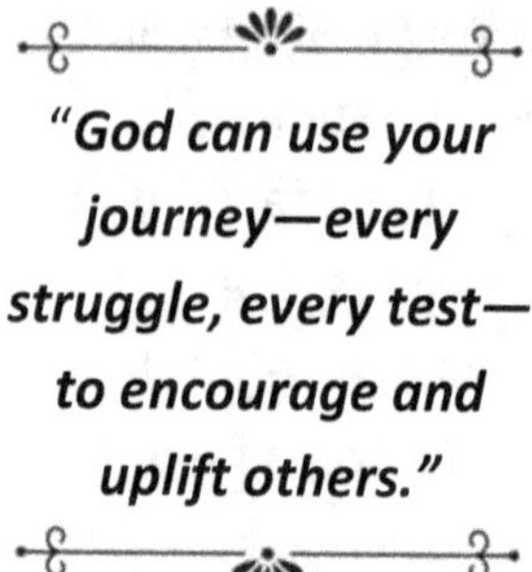

"God can use your journey—every struggle, every test—to encourage and uplift others."

No matter how hard life tests you, keep standing. Keep fighting. Your breakthrough is closer than you think, and when it comes, it will be exactly what you need. You are no longer the person they used to know—and that's the most powerful place you can be.

The Battles in My Mind

After all the excitement of graduating from outpatient, moving into a new place, and finally feeling some peace, life looked perfect on the outside. I was able to purchase yet another car—now I had two—still had my good job, I was single, and no one was stressing me out. No one was chasing me, and I wasn't chasing anyone. I was giving myself time to reset after everything I'd been through. Your girl felt like she was finally free. I thought I had arrived.

I was clean. I had a beautiful home. I opened my doors for holiday dinners, for Thanksgiving, for Christmas. I kept my house immaculate—something I couldn't fully manage when I was using, because honestly, I would rather get high than clean my house. My family looked at me during these gatherings, outings, and celebrations, and constantly told me how much I had grown and how proud they were of me. Even my son—he was smiling, happy to see the woman I was becoming.

By this point, I had been clean and sober for about a year. From the outside, it looked like a success story—and in many ways, it was. But deep down, I knew the truth: The patterns of addiction don't just vanish because the substance is gone. I hadn't fully closed all the doors to my past, and some things were still creeping in. Even though I was no longer addicted to drugs, I found myself addicted to other things that hadn't been dealt with: attention, affection, someone to be next to me, validation in ways that had nothing to do with love.

I didn't see it at first. I thought that because I was done with the substance, everything else would automatically leave with it. But I still had the mindset of an addict—and let me tell y'all exactly what that means: the manipulation, the emotional highs and lows, the need to be needed. I hadn't brought drugs into my new home, but I brought the same behaviors in a different form.

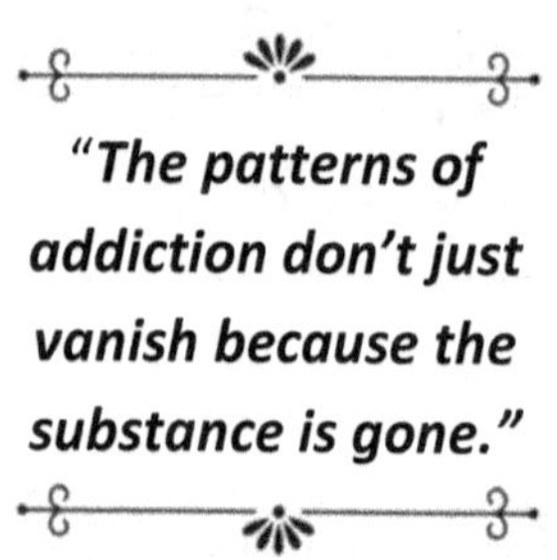

Freedom isn't just about walking away from what hurts you. Freedom is about healing the parts of yourself that allowed you to accept it in the first place. That part, I was still working on. Lord, help my mind—because that was all I had known for years.

This was a different kind of battle. It wasn't about a substance. It was the battle of my mind. The battle of acceptance. The battle for attention. The battle for

validation. The battle with anxious attachment patterns. The battle with rejection. The battle with old programming and habits that had stayed alive in subtle ways. It was exhausting, invisible, and relentless—a fight I had to wage within myself every single day.

Even in my "freedom," the work was far from over. I learned quickly that healing the mind, the heart, and the soul is an ongoing process. Recovery isn't just about removing the thing that hurt you; it's about rebuilding the parts of you that hurt in the first place. And that rebuilding? That's the hardest battle of all.

Chapter 17

When Freedom Isn't Enough

Even though I was still living sober from drugs, I found myself quietly slipping back into old patterns. I began attaching to ex-lovers, entertaining different distractions, hoping they would somehow notice the change in me.

Mind you, I've always said I was a people pleaser, right? So by this time—because I was free from drugs—I wanted everybody to notice. I wanted the accolades and the applause. I wanted them to see and respect the new version of Charmayne—healed, growing, different.

But deep down, I knew many of them, maybe even all of them, could care less. As long as I was still a version of me that gave them free access whenever they wanted, they didn't care about my healing. They wanted what they'd always gotten from me—my body, my time, my energy, my money—because I was a giver.

And when I say I was a giver, I was a giver. I didn't care what the situation or circumstance was—I was always willing to give. I'm not saying that to brag or boast; that's just who I am by nature. They wanted what I was so quick and eager to give, hoping it would lead to something real

. . . but it never did.

See, dealing with low self-esteem will leave you repeating
cycles and patterns that feel almost impossible to
escape—like being stuck in a grave you can't climb out of.
You know how we get—women and men alike—we're
quick to say, "Oh, I got options." But let's be real: Deep
down, we know those options don't want anything more
from us than what they're already getting. They're not
trying to commit. They're not trying to see us for who we
really are. They don't want us—they want what they can
get from us, what they can benefit from.

Nine times out of ten, those "options" are broken and
damaged. They don't want anything more than what
you're willing to give them. That's why saying you have
options isn't really a flex—because sometimes, those
options only come when you're an easy door to walk
through.

And yet, we still entertain it.

Yes, I was in recovery from drugs, no doubt. I was speaking
to people about addiction, healing, and deliverance. I was
visiting rehabs and even asked to speak at a program
center in Delaware. I was sharing my story in different
atmospheres—even in churches. God was using me as a
vessel, and doors were opening.

I was telling my story on the streets to people who were struggling. Some would come up to me and say that every time they looked at me, I gave them a sense of hope. They'd say they were proud of me.

And you know what? In recovery, you start to look different—you have that glow about you. I heard that a lot. I was even helping people get into rehab, taking them there, dropping them off, helping them find housing— whatever I could do. And I'm not saying that for attention or praise, because the Word says that what I do in secret, God will reward openly.

So, I wasn't seeking applause for doing what I knew I was called to do. I just felt good because I was clean—and I was vocal about it.

When you're out there getting high, you don't care who sees you. You don't care that you're looking a hot mess, begging, pleading, degrading yourself. But this time, I wanted people to see me standing tall in recovery—and meaning it.

However, even in all that purpose, I was still crying on the inside.

I didn't understand why I was still suffering. Why was I still carrying wounds that drugs had never touched? I had given up the addiction to substances, but I hadn't yet surrendered the addiction to attention, validation, or love.

I had to keep asking myself why.

The truth was, I had only given God half of me. We never dealt with the root of the problem. I felt Him tugging at me—whispering in my heart, reminding me that true freedom isn't halfway.

> "I had given up the addiction to substances, but I hadn't yet surrendered the addiction to attention, validation, or love."

He wanted all of me—my heart, my body, my relationships, my decisions. But I was still wrestling, still clinging to broken versions of love, still trying to convince myself I was whole when parts of me were still fractured.

The real problem was I wasn't ready to let go—not yet. I hadn't surrendered completely. And if I truly wanted freedom, just like I had been tired of drugs, I would have been able to surrender these other addictions too.

So there I was—a walking testimony of recovery, yet still in need of recovery in other ways. I had cleaned up my body, my habits, my choices—but my heart was still in process.

I thought I was free . . . but I was only halfway there.

Chapter 18

Redirection, Not Rejection

A lot of things in my life started to change when I chose recovery. I began getting serious about multiple areas—working on my credit, taking small steps toward financial stability. I even opened a bank account with a credit union for the first time, and I actually had money sitting in there. That felt like a huge win—something I didn't take for granted.

My relationship with God was still a journey. My relationship with myself was still a journey. Some days I felt close to Him; other days, distant. But even in the distraction, I was still reaching, still trying, still believing He was with me.

The truth was, I still wanted to do things in my own strength. I never really liked being told what to do even as a kid, and as a kid I said when I got older, nobody was going to tell me what to do. But hell, who am I to fight against God?

I'd always carried the pain of being hurt and rejected for so long that I built walls to block everything out. I even tried to block God out.

But no matter how high I built those walls, no matter how much I tried to push Him away, God never left. He never stopped whispering, nudging, calling me forward. And the truth is . . . those walls were only keeping me from the life He was trying to give me. They weren't protecting me—they were trapping me.

Every rejection I thought I'd suffered, every heartbreak and disappointment, every "no" that cut deep . . . was part of a bigger plan I couldn't yet see. And even when I wanted to shut it all down, I felt a pull I couldn't explain—a quiet, unshakable reminder that He was still there, still working, still shaping me.

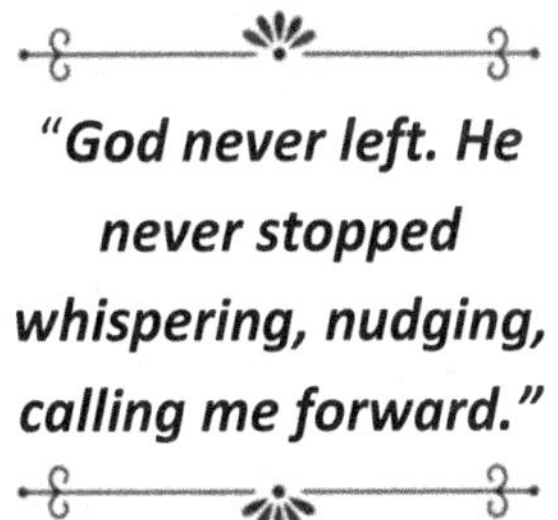

"God never left. He never stopped whispering, nudging, calling me forward."

At the apartment I had been living in, it was a one-bedroom. I let my son have the bedroom, and I took over the living room. I was desiring something bigger and better for me, my son, and my fur baby, Sofie. I wanted a space that reflected the growth I was experiencing with God and with myself.

I started applying for other houses. One place, in particular, looked so promising—I could feel it was going to happen. Everything seemed to be lining up: my job, my credit, all the debt I had paid off, and even my legal matters cleared. I felt like it was already mine.

I made the decision not to renew my lease at my current apartment. We were packing with the expectation of moving into the next chapter of my life.

But somehow . . . it didn't happen.
The enemy can be crafty, but God is clever. What the enemy meant for harm, God would turn around for good. The deal fell through. Everything I thought was certain unraveled right in front of me. With my lease already ended and no place to go, I had to move in with my brother.

The excuse? My credit wasn't good enough, and they flagged an eviction—even though I had proof that everything was a clean slate. I was disappointed. Pissed. Hell yeah, I was. How could people promise something and then take it away? I guess that's life.

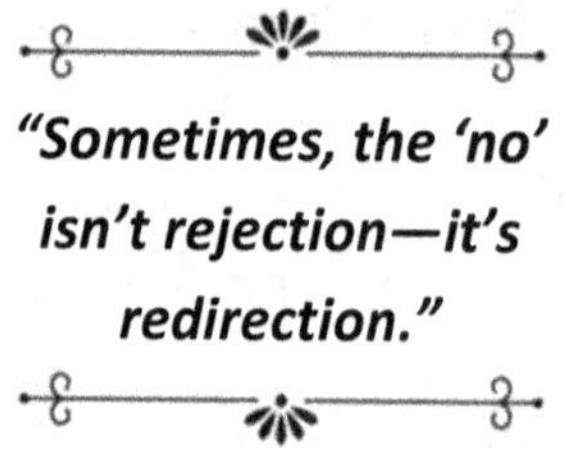

"Sometimes, the 'no' isn't rejection—it's redirection."

Even so, deep in my heart, I had a sense of peace. I was confused, but I knew God had a plan. He was up to something bigger than I could see. I didn't have all the answers, but I had peace—the kind of peace that comes from trusting God even when the circumstances doesn't make sense.

Sometimes, the "no" isn't rejection—it's redirection.

And I was about to find out why my life had felt like a roller coaster for so long. If I'm honest, it wasn't different things tripping me up—it was the same pattern, showing up in different forms.

Little did I know . . . this turn of events was only the beginning. What I thought was a setback was actually setting me up for something I couldn't yet imagine. And God was about to show me that sometimes, the path we resist the most is the one that leads to exactly where we're meant to be.

I didn't know it yet, but the next chapter of my life was going to demand a level of surrender I had never experienced before . . .

Chapter 19

Lessons in Detours

As we were getting ready to move into my brother's house, I had a U-Haul parked out front. I was giving things away, paying people to help, and just ready to get out of that area. Moving in with my brother wasn't part of the plan, but life has a way of rerouting us to the exact place we need to be—even when it doesn't look like what we imagined.

Because I needed somewhere to stay, I had to let go of my pride. Sometimes, we get so caught up in trying to look strong that we forget it's okay to need help. I used to feel embarrassed to ask for anything, thinking I always had to appear like I had it all together. That's been me most of my life—trying too hard to make things look good on the outside even when I was falling apart on the inside. I've always been a people pleaser, like I've said before throughout this whole story. I wanted everyone to see me as strong, capable, and put together, even when I wasn't.

But this time, I decided to embrace the situation with gratitude. I humbled myself and reminded my heart that needing help doesn't make me weak—it makes me human.

I kept searching for my own place. Years before, I had applied for Section 8 housing, but every time I checked the waiting list, it felt like a never-ending story. On one list, I was number 2,000; on another, 3,000. It was discouraging, exhausting, and sometimes just plain heartbreaking. But even in that, God was still making a way. He opened financial doors, provided opportunities, and reminded me that even when things feel stuck, movement is still happening—just in ways we can't always see.

And then, out of nowhere, came another lesson—one that showed up wearing a familiar face. It wasn't someone from my past, but someone in my hometown. The connection felt easy, comforting, and safe. Sometimes we mistake comfort for peace, but comfort can also be a test in disguise. Deep down, I knew I shouldn't have gotten involved with this person because of who they were connected to. Something in my spirit told me to be still, but my heart wanted to believe it would be different. And even though I knew better, I still went along with it. That's the thing about being human—we don't always listen to the whisper until the lesson gets louder.

I started asking myself some hard questions: *Why do I keep repeating certain cycles? Am I really loving myself the way I say I am? Have I done the full work of healing—or just enough to get by?* The truth was, I hadn't fully. And that's okay. Healing isn't about perfection—it's about awareness. It's about recognizing when old habits are trying to sneak their way back in and choosing differently this time.

Healing isn't a straight path. Sometimes the lessons we need most come dressed as distractions, challenges, or temporary comforts. But those moments aren't failures—they're invitations. Invitations to realign with your purpose, to strengthen your boundaries, and to remember who you are when no one else is around.

That's what this season taught me: Every detour carries purpose. Every setback holds a lesson. Every distraction is a reminder to return to your healing, your goals, and your truth. Growth requires patience, and healing requires humility. You have to trust the process, even when you don't understand it. Life's twists and turns aren't meant to break you—they're meant to shape you. Every detour is a step toward becoming the person you were always meant to be.

One night, this person took me out to eat. We laughed, talked, and for a few hours, everything felt easy. Some nights, we'd just sit in the car talking for hours, sharing our fears, frustrations, and dreams until we fell asleep right there. Other times, they'd stay the night, and we'd just vibe—no pressure, no pretending. It felt good to have that kind of comfort again.

But see, I'm the type of person that when I open up, I really open up. I talk too much sometimes. I put too much of my business out there, and I've learned the hard way that not everyone can be trusted with that kind of access. That's something I'm still learning—to protect my peace and my story.

Even in that comfort, I had to remind myself that familiarity doesn't always equal growth. Comfort isn't always confirmation. Sometimes, it's a test to see if you've really learned what you say you have.

Every relationship brings its own lessons—arguments, misunderstandings, moments that test your patience—but the real test isn't how you show up for them, it's how you show up for you.

This chapter of my life wasn't about blame or regret—it was about awareness. It was about realizing that even the detours, the distractions, and the delays are all part of God's design. Growth comes in detours. Strength comes from humility. And true healing comes when you finally choose yourself first.

Chapter 20

Shadows of Wanting

At this point in my life, it felt like I was finally proving something to myself. Doors were opening—approvals, opportunities, even housing—I got approved to move, even when I knew I was still number 2,000 or 3,000 on the waiting list. Somehow, God made a way. And yes, I also got approved for weight loss surgery. I won't lie, it wasn't just about health. Part of me wanted it because I was still wrestling with insecurities, still trying to feel beautiful, still trying to feel enough. I thought maybe if I changed how I looked, I'd somehow be treated differently, seen differently, loved differently. I've always had a pretty face, I just wanted the body to match. I wasn't going to the gym consistently—I just wanted the easy fix.

Even in the middle of all this progress, God was showing up. Grace and mercy were flowing. He was reminding me that He was still reaching for me, even while I was distracted by someone I loved so deeply. And when I say deeply, I mean the kind of love that grabs your soul, makes you want to give everything—even at the expense of your own peace.

This individual was the first I had never cheated on—or

even had the desire to. There was something about him that kept me tethered. I don't know if it was love, control, or just the pattern of wanting to be needed, but I was all-in. I even distanced myself from a close friend of twenty-seven years—the same one who had helped me in my recovery journey—just to keep the peace, to try to be the woman I thought he deserved. I was still trapped in people-pleasing, still trying to prove that I was the "better" woman—the ride-or-die, the one who could love harder, bend without breaking, and always be enough.

We do this sometimes, don't we? Bend over backward to impress, to be chosen, to feel like we've earned someone's love. Ignore red flags. Silence our pain. Convince ourselves that trying harder will make someone finally see our worth. That was me. Chasing validation. Trying to prove I was enough, even when my heart, my energy, and my self-respect were screaming that it was too much.

Even through it all, I didn't fully let go. I carried him with me into my new space—the home I finally got approved for, outside the county I grew up in. Even though I knew he was still entertaining other options, I told myself it didn't matter. I loved him. I really did. I wanted to be the one. I wanted it so badly that I ignored the quiet warnings my spirit kept whispering.

And just as before, the patterns returned. The disrespect. The inconsistency. The lack of boundaries. And there I was again, sitting with that familiar ache—not enough.

That's when it hit me: The person I brought into my life wasn't the entire problem. The real lesson was in the version of me I carried—the old insecurities, the anxious attachment, the people-pleasing, the need to prove myself. Healing wasn't about changing them or controlling them. Healing was about looking inward, loving myself, and giving attention to the parts of me that had been neglected for far too long.

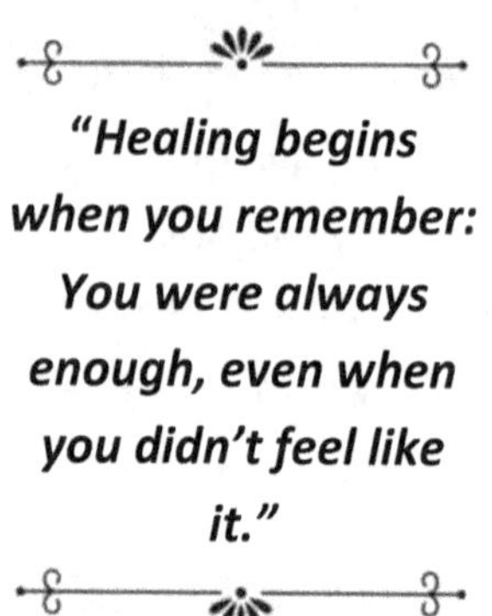

"Healing begins when you remember: You were always enough, even when you didn't feel like it."

Sometimes I sit back now, listening to my own story, and I have to laugh and shake my head. Foolish, yes—but every misstep was a lesson. And still is. Every moment of feeling not enough was really a call—to remember my worth, reclaim my power, protect my boundaries.

That's the truth I'm still learning: Growth comes not from the people we hope will choose us, but from the love we learn to give ourselves, even in the shadows of wanting. Even when your heart aches, even when your mind questions, even when you carry someone else into a space meant for your peace. Healing begins when you remember: You were always enough, even when you didn't feel like it.

And oh, beautiful soul, that realization—bittersweet as it is—is powerful. Because even in the shadows of wanting, God was still showing up, teaching me, reminding me, and shaping me into the woman I was always meant to be.

Chapter 21

Surrender

At this point, I knew God was getting tired of me—heck, I was getting tired of me too. It felt like I was going through a revolving door, the same cycles over and over again. I kept wondering, *When will I ever learn? When will I ever get it right?* God had been wanting to save me from me for a long time. But I kept running. I've been known for avoiding my problems instead of facing them head-on. And because God doesn't go against our will, His hands were tied—He couldn't fully save me from myself while I kept resisting. I would give Him some of me, but not all of me. I'd surrender a part of myself and then try to take it back.

"God had been wanting to save me from me for a long time."

The Bible says, "A double-minded man is unstable in all his ways" (James 1:8 KJV).

I've always been told I was a smart individual—that I can get things done. Show me how to do something once, and I'll figure it out. I'll hit the ground running—no hesitation, no second thoughts. I know how to make things happen business-wise; however, I haven't fully mastered it yet. I know my way around to get things done, but I just don't fully utilize my potential.

And then there are some days that fear grips me, and I hold myself back. Then I become scared and lose confidence when things don't work out the way I would hope they would, or believe they should have. On the other hand, when it came to handling relationships and caring for myself mentally, I was dumb as a doorknob at times.

But I look back a lot of the times, and I feel like I should have been further in life—or even had a career by now. I went back to college, not for hair, but for human services this time. I had my classes and everything lined up, but uncertainty made me back out. I knew I would have done well because I genuinely enjoy helping people.

This is why I believe God wants to save me from myself—because He's tired of me self-sabotaging. There are people out here who need my help, people I'm supposed to reach, touch, and inspire. But before I can truly help save others, He needs to save me first. He wants to get me out of my own way, to heal me, strengthen me, and prepare me for what's ahead.

Again, it's not about the destination—it's about the journey. That's where we learn the lessons we need. And even though I've stumbled and doubted myself, I now see that God has been working on me the whole time, shaping me into who I was always meant to be.

As I tried to balance a relationship at the same time as trying to balance my new beginning, it started becoming exhausting. All the while, things in my life were still flowing abundantly—the opportunities, the blessings, my progress—but in this relationship that I was still entangled in, the disrespect started coming in from all angles from this individual, until I was reminded of why I had to fully let him go.

Then came the final straw. I wanted control. You know how it goes—if you look for something, you'll find it. And I did.

I went on this guy's social media because I wanted to see why he was distant, why he wasn't calling or reaching out. I asked if there was someone else, and he would say no— but I found out there was always somebody, whether he showed me or I discovered it myself the hard way.

What I saw broke my heart. It felt like I couldn't breathe. My heart was racing so fast I could taste the blood in my mouth. I thought I was going to pass out and die.

Even then, I didn't completely leave this man alone. I still wanted to hold on, and he still held on to me. I loved him—I can't lie and say I didn't. But the truth is, the damage was done. You try to overlook everything—even becoming delusional to the fact that you *know* it's not good.

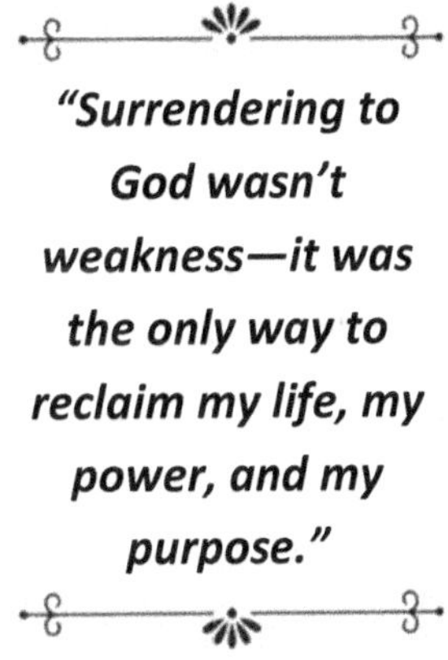

"Surrendering to God wasn't weakness—it was the only way to reclaim my life, my power, and my purpose."

It sounded crazy, but I had to come to the realization that I needed to surrender completely—because this individual had too much power over me. God was showing me that He had been trying to protect me, not from others, but from the version of myself that couldn't set boundaries, that didn't love herself enough to say no.

I also realized things weren't working because I had made this flawed man my god. My heartbreak became a turning point. For years, God had been calling me, but I finally answered. I was tired of being hurt, tired of being overlooked, tired of hurting myself. I realized that surrendering to God wasn't weakness—it was the only way to reclaim my life, my power, and my purpose.

Even with all the trauma and the triggers I relived while writing this book, I knew I had to share my story—not for approval or sympathy, but because someone needed to hear it. I needed to write it for myself, for my son, and for anyone walking through a similar path.

Along the way, I witnessed something beautiful. Through my journey of sobriety, I watched my son graduate, win his first football championship, buy his first car and pay it off, hold a good job—all while I stood five years clean.

I thank God for every high and every low. Healing isn't perfect. Growth isn't linear. Every day is a step forward, even when it feels like two steps back. I'm learning to embrace my imperfections, to love myself through the ugly, the pain, the disappointments, and the heartbreaks. I'm learning accountability—acknowledging where I was the problem, and owning my role in the relationships and choices I made.

Because truth is, I still struggle sometimes. I still have moments where I chase love in the wrong places, or seek validation where I shouldn't. That may sound hypocritical to some, but it's real—because I'm still learning. I'm still growing.

While facing my traumas and the truth of who I was and who I am becoming, God kept showing me that I was loved. He kept showing me His grace and His mercy—all the while still saying, "My child, why do you keep choosing pain, thinking it's love? I see your strength. I love you. Let Me save you from you."

Healing is a choice, my love—
and I finally said yes. Yes to
being safe from myself.

I'm still being processed. I'm still
being taken through the fire,
because I haven't mastered it yet. But I've said yes to
God's love, His grace, and His purpose.

Even though I still have my struggles—my thorn in the
side, like Paul— I know God is turning my pain into
purpose.

> **"I know God is turning my pain into purpose."**

Chapter 22

Maintaining Recovery

Recovery became more than just staying clean and sober for me—it became a complete lifestyle change. I had to learn to leave behind certain people, places, and things that no longer aligned with the life I was praying for. It was not easy, and some days still are not.

What truly began changing my life was seeking God wholeheartedly. In my weakest moments, I cried out to Him for strength, guidance, peace, and healing. I still do. I am not perfect, and I do not pretend to have everything figured out, but recovery remains one of my main focuses every single day.

I am still standing. I am still fighting. I am still loving people and still helping others even while continuing my own healing journey. That, to me, is strength.

Through faith, God began opening doors for me mentally, emotionally, and spiritually. I now spend much of my time encouraging others, praying with people, helping those in need, and sharing my story without shame. If someone is hungry, I try to feed them. If someone has nowhere to stay, I try to help however I can, even if it means using what little I have to get them shelter for a night or connect them with resources.

I never look down on people who are still struggling because I know what it feels like to fight battles silently. I understand pain, addiction, disappointment, and survival. That is why I choose compassion over judgment.

Today, I am walking toward becoming a recovery advocate—the voice for those who are ashamed to speak up. My life is proof that God can restore, rebuild, and renew a person who once felt broken.

If my story reaches even one person who feels hopeless, then every painful chapter I survived will have had a purpose.

Recommendation

If you are struggling, my first recommendation is to find a quiet place where you can sit with your thoughts and breathe. Healing begins in stillness. Seek God in whatever way you understand Him—through prayer, honesty, or simply asking for help. And if your faith feels distant right now, you are still not alone. Healing is still possible for you.

I also encourage you to reach out for professional support such as a counselor, recovery program, or trusted mental health resource. Strength is not found in isolation—it is found in connection, guidance, and truth. If there is someone in your life you truly trust, allow yourself to lean on them. And if not, there are safe spaces and people trained to help you carry what feels too heavy right now— to give you the tools you need to overcome the brokenness and negative thinking.

This journey will not be easy, and healing does not happen overnight. But change is possible for anyone with a made-up mind and a purposeful heart, or even a broken heart that is sincere about change. The Bible reminds us that God is near to the brokenhearted and sees the intentions of the heart. So give it to Him—cast your cares upon Him, for He cares for you (1 Peter 5:7).

And if you choose to pray, it does not have to be fancy words. Simply be honest. Just speak as if you were talking to a friend. Tell God where you are and ask Him to help you. Ask Him to come into your life, into your heart, and guide you. Ask for strength in the areas where you feel powerless—whether it is addiction, pain, trauma, or struggle. Ask Him to be Lord over your life and to lead you into healing and change.

You are not too far gone, and your story is not over. Step by step, moment by moment, you can rebuild your life. And I hope my story reminds you that even in brokenness, purpose can still be born.

In His Pain, He Became Purpose-Driven

My son, Cyn'Cere, did receive love, support, and guidance while coping with everything he experienced and witnessed. Like many people trying to process pain, he searched for ways to cope, and at times that included using marijuana as an escape from emotions he struggled to carry. But even through that, he never lost who he truly was at his core.

Today, he expresses himself through writing and music, using his voice and creativity as an outlet for healing. He has also grown closer to God, and watching his faith develop has been one of the most beautiful parts of our journey. He is currently building his own fashionable clothing brand and working toward becoming an entrepreneur.

Despite everything he has been through, he remains loving, respectful, and inspiring to those around him. Cyn'Cere's story is still being written, but I am proud of the young man he continues to become.

Closing Words

I pray my journey inspires, comforts, and frees someone reading this. You are not alone. I hope it reminds you that you are enough, you are capable, you are loved—and no matter how long it takes, God's timing is perfect. Healing starts with surrender.

So don't be so hard on yourself, but forgive yourself for what you didn't know.

Forgive others.

And remember: *Your story matters. YOU matter.*

You are still beautiful . . . flaws and all.

- Connect with the author -

For questions, speaking engagements, or to share your thoughts about the book, you can reach me at
harrellcharmayne@gmail.com

Special Shout-Out

To my relatives—you know who you are. Your love, your support, and even your tough love has spoken louder than words ever could. To my son's goddad—thank you for everything, my love; thank you for holding us up when we were down and the knowledge you've given me through this journey. And to everyone who played a part in raising my boy—thank you for taking time, for showing up, and for never judging me along this journey.

I am grateful for each and every one of you—the ones who pushed me, the ones who challenged me, and even those who seemed hard on me, because all of it shaped me. And to those who said I'd never be nothing, to those who made me feel like I was actually nothing, even those who literally spat in my face and on me—I thank you too. I used all of that as fuel to go forward because I knew you saw something great in me. That's why it felt like your demons tried to destroy me, but God used it to build me. I thank God for those who had faith in me, even when I didn't have faith in myself.

I couldn't have done this without my village. I couldn't have grown without the love, the lessons, and the truth you all carried me with. From the bottom of my heart, I thank you all.

www.ingramcontent.com/pod-product-compliance
Lightning Source LLC
Chambersburg PA
CBHW071444130726
47997CB00006B/2217